GREY'S ANATOMY 101

D1166768

VISUAL & PERFORMING ARTS

OTHER TITLES IN THE SMART POP SERIES

GREY'S ANATOMY 101

SEATTLE GRACE, UNAUTHORIZED

Edited by Leah Wilson
VISUAL & PERFORMING ARTS

BENBELLA BOOKS, INC.
Dallas, Texas

"I Want to Write for *Grey's*" © 2007 by Kristin Harmel
"If Addison Hadn't Returned, Would Derek and Meredith Have Made It as a Couple?"
    © 2007 by Carly Phillips
"Why Drs. Grey and Shepherd Will Never Live Happily Ever After" © 2007 by
    Elizabeth Engstrom
"'We Don't Do Well with Mothers Here'" © 2007 by Beth Macias
"*Grey's Anatomy* and the New Man" © 2007 by Todd Gilchrist
"Diagnostic Notes, Case Histories, and Profiles of Acute Hybridity in *Grey's Anatomy*"
    © 2007 by Sarah Wendell
"Sex in Seattle" © 2007 by Jacqueline Carey
"Love Stinks" © 2007 by Eileen Rendahl
"Drawing the Line" © 2007 by Janine Hiddlestone
"Brushing Up on Your Bedside Manner" © 2007 by Erin Dailey
"Finding the Hero" © 2007 by Lawrence Watt-Evans
"Next of Kin" © 2007 by Melissa Rayworth
"Only the Best for Cristina Yang" © 2007 by Robert Greenberger
"What Would Bailey Do?" © 2007 by Lani Diane Rich
"Walking a Thin Line" © 2007 by Tanya Michna
"Shades of Grey" © 2007 by Yvonne Jocks
"Anatomy of Twenty-First Century Television" © 2007 by Kevin Smokler
Additional Materials © BenBella Books, Inc.

BenBella Books, Inc.
6440 N. Central Expressway, Suite 617
Dallas, TX 75206
www.benbellabooks.com
Send feedback to feedback@benbellabooks.com

Printed in the United States of America
10 9 8 7 6 5 4 3 2 1

Library of Congress Cataloging-in-Publication Data

Grey's anatomy 101 : Seattle Grace, unauthorized / edited by Leah Wilson.
    p. cm.
ISBN 1-933771-14-3
1. Grey's anatomy (Television program) I. Wilson, Leah.

PN1992.77.G698 2007
791.45'72--dc22

2007016643

Proofreading by Emily Chauvier and Yara Abuata
Cover design by Allison Bard
Text design and composition by Laura Watkins
Printed by Bang Printing

Distributed by Independent Publishers Group
To order call (800) 888-4741
www.ipgbook.com

For special sales contact Yara Abuata at yara@benbellabooks.com

TABLE OF CONTENTS

We all have our dream jobs: movie star, fireman, cardiothoracic surgeon. Kristin Harmel wants to write for *Grey's*. And what's not to like? The writers seem like they'd be a blast to work with, and you could see McDreamy pretty much whenever you wanted. But Kristin has more than just a dream. Kristin has *qualifications*.

Kristin Harmel

I WANT TO WRITE FOR *GREY'S*

Ms. Shonda Rhimes
Executive Producer and Series Creator
Grey's Anatomy
Prospect Avenue
Los Angeles, CA 90027

Dear Ms. Rhimes,

I want to write for *Grey's*. Sure, I know you must get applications from people all the time. I mean, who *wouldn't* want to get inside Meredith's head and make decisions for her? Who wouldn't want to write Derek's character and make him choose Meredith from the start? Who wouldn't want to help straighten out the interns' love lives and bring the loveable Denny back to life?

So why, you might be asking, should you pick me? Why should you choose me? Why should you love me? Well, it's not just because I badly paraphrase your main characters' memorable words in application letters. It's because I have a real passion for your show. I am nearly obsessed with the characters who live in your head. And I have a wealth of my own bizarre dating and relating experiences that I could bring to bear upon Mere, Izzie, George, Cristina, Alex, Derek, and the whole staff at Seattle Grace. (After all, I figure I might as well make all my romantic failures count for *something*.)

Before *Grey's Anatomy* debuted, I didn't realize that being cheated on, having complex family issues, and marinating in my own insecurity would qualify me for a job. I didn't guess that getting into almost unbelievable romantic entanglements would make me the perfect writer for your show. But here's the thing. They do. Because if there's one thing I know, it's how to make a mess of my life. And then laugh at it. I'd like to do the same for the gang at Seattle Grace. I think that's largely what *Grey's Anatomy* is all about: Life falls apart, but your characters still manage to find humor in the everyday and solace in each other.

So without further ado, in lieu of a résumé, I will tell you why I, a novelist who won't answer the phone or have any human contact whatsoever whenever a *Grey's* episode is airing on ABC, would be the perfect addition to your writing staff.

After all, I'm Meredith with a writing degree instead of a medical one.

2

REASON #1 TO HIRE ME: I AM A FLAWED MESS

Okay, so usually this would not be considered a major selling point on a job application. In fact, my initial instinct would be to bury my flaws. But for you, Ms. Rhimes, I fly my mess flag high. Why, might you ask? Well, it seems to be the thing to do, at least in the fictional world in which your characters dwell. Meredith, Izzie, Cristina, Alex, and George are all proud to be the messes they are. They wear their insecurities and their faults on their sleeves like others wear their hearts. I kind of like that. I've spent a lifetime hiding my insecurities beneath the surface. Why not let them be part of who I am? Especially since my flaws make me that much more qualified to write for your show. After all, isn't *Grey's* based on the tenet that people's flaws shape and drive them?

One of the best things about *Grey's Anatomy* is that none of the characters are perfect; they all have glaring imperfections. They're not imperfect in a comical way, like *Friends's* divorce-prone Ross, brainless Joey, or formerly fat Monica. They're not like *Desperate Housewives's* promiscuous

Gabby, frigid Bree, or scattered Susan. No, the characters on *Grey's Anatomy*—particularly Meredith—are flawed in a real way. As you yourself have said, Ms. Rhimes, "Meredith is the one of only a few women on television who is truly flawed. FLAWED in capital letters."

Meredith is too insecure and self-questioning. George is too passive. Cristina is too pushy and driven. Izzie is too emotional, and haunted by questions. Alex is too immature. Derek is too conflicted to commit. Addison has made mistakes that are too big to recover from. Burke is too much of a perfectionist. The Chief is too focused on work. And Dr. Bailey is all too human.

"FLAWED in capital letters" only scratches the surface of problems that run true and deep in this complicated cast of characters.

Well, guess what: I'm FLAWED in capital letters, too. Actually, to be more specific, I'm FLAWED in capital letters and then underlined. Probably italicized, too. And who better to get inside your characters' heads than the Queen of Flaws? (That would be me, by the way. I've just crowned myself.)

Ask anyone who knows me. They might be nice about it at first, but loosen them up with a martini or two and they'll spill the truth.

"Kristin Harmel is a mess," they'll tell you. "A flawed mess. We love her just the same, but yeah, she sure knows how to make a disaster out of her life."

Never was this as clear to me as it was the night *Grey's Anatomy* premiered.

Like many other people, I watched the first episode of the first season back in March 2005 expecting to sort of like the show. It sounded intriguing. However, when Meredith woke up naked next to a rather dreamy guy named Derek and awkwardness ensued, I sat up a little straighter in my chair.

"Wait a minute," I said to myself. (Because I often talk to myself while watching TV alone. It's very sad, really.) "I've been there."

Well, not *there* exactly. (Because if I woke up next to Patrick Dempsey, I probably wouldn't make him leave. In fact, I'd probably lock him in my bedroom and keep him there forever. Is that wrong? . . . Ahem. . . .) What I mean is, *there* in terms of waking up next to someone I really shouldn't have been waking up next to. Being in a hurry to get him out the door.

Feeling mortified as the bright morning light pours in my window and the haze of the night before has worn off. (Although, of course, in case you happen to talk to my mom, I hadn't actually *slept with* the aforementioned unintentional overnight guest. Just, er, did some heavy making out. Just thought I'd note that.)

"Wait a minute," I said to myself again as I continued to watch that first episode. (Because I not only talk to myself but often frequently repeat myself. Yes, I know, I should seek professional help.) "This all sounds very familiar."

By the end of the episode, I was in love. Why? It wasn't just McDreamy's deliciously sexy dimples or his run-your-fingers-through-it-perfect hair (although that didn't hurt). It was because unlike many fictional TV or movie accounts of a one-night stand, this one was messy. Meredith was a mess. She'd gotten herself into quite the scrape. And against the grain of TV tradition, there wasn't going to be a miraculous, one-hour TV fix to this one. Meredith had accidentally slept with her boss. And there would be no happily-ever-after.

I was hooked. It was *real*.

4

To my absolute delight, in the coming weeks, the characters got themselves into one romantic scrape after another. Of course they did. As my good friend Sarah, also a chick-lit author like me, recently said, *"Grey's Anatomy* is chick-lit! On TV!" And what good is chick-lit without romantic disaster? Just ask Bridget Jones. Or her McDreamy, Mark Darcy.

Well, let me tell you, Shonda Rhimes—if you're looking for a new source for flaws and romantic disaster for the coming seasons, I'm your girl. Romantic Disaster is my middle name. Really. Kristin Romantic-Disaster Harmel. Feel free to call me "McDisaster" if that rolls off the tongue better.

I am the master of coming up with silly nicknames for people, such as Deputy McLove (for my friend's police officer boyfriend), Flight Boy (for a fighter-jet flying ex), and Saxy McSax (for a sexy saxophone player I dated).

I've unwittingly gone on a date with a married man who only later told me that he was not, in fact, single (a fact that I might have been able to pick up on had he actually been wearing a wedding ring any of the times I saw him). Doesn't this scream Meredith?

I've had the unique misfortune of being cheated on twice in nearly back-to-back relationships. That should get me into Derek's head, right?

I've been the wimpy pushover in a relationship (George, anybody?). I've single-handedly screwed relationships up (à la Alex). I've been in relationships where both the guy and I were in very ambitious stages of our lives (hello, Cristina and Burke!). Sadly, I've even had someone I loved very much die (which puts me right up there in Izzie's head).

But oh no, it doesn't stop there. I have a whole list of experiences that you haven't even thrown the Seattle Grace gang into yet.

Finding out that my new flame actually has a one-year-old son he has neglected to mention for the entire year I've known him? Check.

Being basically stalked by a major league ballplayer? Yep.

Having a roller-coaster fling that turned into a one-year relationship with a minor rock star? Been there, done that.

So clearly my background uniquely qualifies me to throw wrenches (or, more appropriately, scalpels and surgical sponges) in the works of everything at Seattle Grace. I'm a Dictionary of Disaster, an Encyclopedia of Errors, a Thesaurus of Theatrical Failures. And before I come up with any more ridiculously bad phrases to describe my vast experience in the area of romantic mishaps, let me go on to my next point.

5

REASON #2 TO HIRE ME: YOU'RE MY SOUL MATE

Sorry, Shonda. Didn't mean to freak you out. I don't mean to say that you personally are my soul mate. No offense; I'm sure you're lovely. It's just that my boyfriend would probably have a problem with me saying that. No, what I mean is that your show is my soul mate show.

I used to think it was *Sex and the City*. And to some extent, it still is. In my own little private fantasy world, I'm Carrie Bradshaw—albeit with cheaper shoes. I thought there would never be another show I'd connect with in such a deep way.

And then you and your *Grey's Anatomy* came along and swept me off my Nine West-clad feet. You had me at hello. I watched with rapt attention as Mere and Derek danced their little metaphorical dance of love. I rooted for Cristina and Burke to get together. I cheered when George found a girlfriend who was most decidedly not Meredith. I sobbed along with Izzie when she lost Denny.

When your characters had their hearts broken, mine broke, too.

When they acted irrationally, I always understood. When they hurt, I hurt. When they were happy, I was happy. I felt like they were an extension of me—my neurotic side (Meredith), my control-freak side (Cristina), my always-optimistic-and-hopeful side (Izzie), my sometimes-passive side (George), and my say-it-like-it-is side (Alex).

Every week, I watch the show with a sort of open-mouthed awe.

"I do that same thing!" I find myself saying over and over again. (Once again, talking to myself. Yes, I know, I'm crazy.) Or, "Oh my goodness, that could be me!"

Okay, so sometimes this is said with just the slightest bit of irrational optimism (as in the scene early in season three in which Meredith found herself in bed between Finn and Derek—I suppose thinking "that could be me" might be just a *teensy bit* unrealistic, as I have never, in fact, found myself sandwiched between Chris O'Donnell and Patrick Dempsey, though I'm working on that). But the sentiment is true; so many of the feelings, the actions, and the reactions of the characters ring true in a way I never knew a television show's could.

Now, instead of wondering if guys are a "Big" or an "Aidan" (à la *Sex and the City*), I now find myself wondering if they're a Derek. Or a McSteamy. Or a Finn. Or a George. Or an Alex. Or, if I'm lucky enough, a Denny with a different fate.

And when I find myself watching Meredith, Cristina, and the others doing things or making mistakes that I myself would make, I feel just a little bit more sane, a little bit more at home, a little bit more like my place in the world makes sense.

I know I'm not the only one who feels this way.

Ms. Rhimes, I know you've said before that Meredith is all of us on our best and worst days. I agree; when I watch her, I feel like I'm watching *me*. She is everything I aspire to be and everything I rue being, all in one. She is "everywoman" in a way that even Carrie Bradshaw never was.

And since she is inside my head, I long to get inside hers.

In fact, I've already started.

REASON #3 TO HIRE ME: I HAVE SOME GREAT ON-THE-JOB EXPERIENCE

They say that experience generally qualifies people for jobs, right? Well, as a professional writer for the last decade, I certainly have the writing part down. As a walking dating-disaster, I've certainly logged the requisite hours in heartbreak and devastation. But what kind of on-the-job experience could put me in Meredith's shoes better than anything else?

How about meeting Derek Shepherd? Hugging Derek Shepherd? Chatting for an hour with Derek Shepherd? Appearing in a photograph (see www.kristinharmel.com) that really makes it look very much like I'm actually *out* with Derek Shepherd?

Okay, okay, so in *real* life, I suppose we'd have to call him Patrick Dempsey if you're going to be a stickler for the whole "reality" and "not living in a fantasy world" thing (sheesh, real life is so boring). But any way you slice it, he's still my—and Meredith's—ideal McDreamy.

The most crucial part of my preparation for the role of *Grey's Anatomy* writer came last spring when I was asked to interview Dempsey (whom I will subsequently refer to as McDreamy, because, well, wouldn't Meredith?) for a magazine article. I had watched the show addictively. I had fallen in love with McDreamy, just like every other woman in America. And I was sure that it would be a quick interview that would leave me wanting more.

But as I settled in next to a very dreamy-looking McDreamy during the Annual Mobil 1 Twelve Hours of Sebring auto race in Florida (of which he was the grand marshal), and the publicist with him told him he had ten minutes with me, he turned to me with a grin.

"Only ten minutes?" he asked with a very McDreamy smile. I nodded, trying not to drool or, perhaps more embarrassingly, throw myself directly onto his lap in hapless lust. "Why don't you stay longer?" he asked. "The race just started, and I'm planning to stay until the end. That's twelve hours from now."

And so I did. Not for twelve hours, because, well, that would have been a little psychotic (not that I'm implying I don't have a screw or two loose, because clearly I do). But we chatted and talked and laughed for an hour (and I even managed to keep the corners of my mouth drool-free the entire time). And although the logical part of my brain reminded me that it was just an interview and that this particular McDreamy was, in fact, very much happily married (darn reality!), I couldn't stop the Meredith inside of me from doing a little happy dance. I was sitting side-by-side with McDreamy. He was looking into my eyes. Laughing at the things I said. Responding enthusiastically to my questions. Asking me to stay longer when I said perhaps I'd better go.

Oh my goodness, McDreamy was looking at me the same way he gazes at Meredith. He had fallen for me!

Okay, okay, that might be a bit of an overstatement. He was probably just being charming and polite and trying to kill an hour during the twelve-hour race. But for sixty minutes, in a press suite at a raceway instead of inside an operating room, I knew exactly what it felt like to be Meredith Grey.

REASON #4 TO HIRE ME: I'LL FIT RIGHT IN IN YOUR WRITERS' ROOM

Finally, after reading the description you once gave of the *Grey's* writers' room, I knew I'd belong. "Our writers' room is super-secret, incredibly crazy, sacred place," you once said. "In that room, we talk, we laugh, we eat a LOT of cupcakes, we jog on the treadmill to burn off those cupcakes, and most importantly, we come up with the storylines for the season and for each episode."

Well, Ms. Rhimes, I am obsessed with cupcakes. In fact, anyone who knows me will tell you that I have a deep-rooted belief that any day that begins with a cupcake is destined to be a good day. (Really, try it sometime. It works. Now if you'll excuse me while I try in vain to button my pants. . . .) I have waited outside Sprinkles Cupcakes on Little Santa Monica Boulevard in Beverly Hills for more than an hour, just for a taste of vanilla on vanilla. I've waited for forty-five minutes for a perfect New York City Magnolia cupcake. I was late for my own book launch party last year because I became obsessed with the idea of scarfing down a Starbucks vanilla cupcake first, only I couldn't find one. And like you, I also jog on the treadmill to burn off those calories.

(Well, more accurately, I stand on the treadmill and *think* about jogging on it. But that's where I get some of my very best ideas for plotting books. Unfortunately, it's not where I do my best calorie-burning.)

See, with the exception of my aversion to treadmill exercise, I'd fit in perfectly in that writers' room that you call your "Narnia" and your

8

"Oz." I love Narnia! I love Oz! I was even Dorothy for Halloween last year! (Don't judge me for trick-or-treating at the age of twenty-seven. I like candy.) I often sing "If I Only Had a Brain" in the shower! (Okay, perhaps I should not have admitted that last part.)

But truly, cupcake obsession and treadmill laziness aside, I am a team player. I am a passionate writer. And there's no place I'd rather create magic than inside your writers' room, with Meredith, Derek, and the rest of your characters right there at my fingertips.

I'm Done with Reasons; Now I'm Just Begging

And so I ask you, Shonda Rhimes, let me climb even further inside Meredith's head. Let me use my own richly ridiculous past to shape the futures of the characters you so expertly created. Let me grieve with Izzie, struggle with George, become a better person with Alex, push the limits with Cristina. Let me further complicate the lives of Dr. Bailey, Dr. Burke, and Addison Montgomery-Shepherd. Let me be part of your team. Let me become one with the gang at Seattle Grace.

Please. Pick me. Choose me. Love me.

Okay, you don't have to love me, exactly. Not yet, anyhow. But at least give me a job. Hey, you don't even have to pay me. If we could arrange for, say, a little kiss from McDreamy every now and then, I think we could work something out. I mean, really, I'm just thinking of the good of the team. Isn't that generous of me? He could probably use some extra practice for his love scenes, right? I'd be happy to be the Meredith stand-in anytime you need me.

I'm just that kind of team player. Maybe if I do really well, we can even arrange for that season three Patrick Dempsey-Chris O'Donnell scenario. What do you think? Sounds like a good holiday bonus to me.

See you in the cupcake room.

Sincerely yours,

Kristin Romantic-Disaster Harmel-Dempsey
(Okay, so *perhaps* that last part was just wishful thinking.)

9

KRISTIN HARMEL is the author of the Warner Books/5 Spot novels *How to Sleep with a Movie Star* and *The Blonde Theory*, as well as the upcoming *The Art of French Kissing* (Warner Books, February 2008) and *When You Wish* (a YA novel from Delacorte Press/Random House, January 2008). She is a frequent contributor to *People* magazine and a freelance writer whose work has appeared in magazines including *Glamour*, *American Baby*, *Men's Health*, and *YM*. She appears regularly on the nationally syndicated TV morning show *The Daily Buzz*. After having lived in New York, Paris, and Los Angeles, she now resides in Orlando, Florida, where she can be found every Thursday night on her couch, her TV tuned to ABC. She really has met Patrick Dempsey and would like to consider changing her name to Kristin Harmel-McDreamy. Visit her Web site at www.KristinHarmel.com.

10

REFERENCES

All Shonda Rhimes quotes from:

Rhimes, Shonda. "*Grey's Anatomy* FAQ." *Grey's Anatomy*. 6 Sep. 2006. <http://games.abc.go.com/primetime/greysanatomy/faq.htm>

It's a well-established pattern: Boy meets girl, boy gets girl, television ratings plummet. Shows have tried all sorts of tricks to maintain audience interest, most of which have involved tearing the new lovers apart and making them work their way back to one another. But often as not, by the time they get there, something feels off. They aren't the same people they were back when they fell in love the first time. Those insurmountable issues that split them up in the first place turn out to actually *be* insurmountable. Something about the relationship just doesn't work. Not so with Derek and Meredith. In fact, their relationship was almost *better* the second time around. Why? Because of Addison.

Carly Phillips

IF ADDISON HADN'T RETURNED, WOULD DEREK AND MEREDITH HAVE MADE IT AS A COUPLE?

From the moment they met, Derek and Meredith were the couple the audience rooted for, the couple they wanted to see end up together. The chemistry between the characters was incredible and they seemed meant to be—up until the moment Derek's *wife* Addison Montgomery-Shepherd arrived at Seattle Grace. Derek's wife. Not his ex-wife or his one-time lover, but his wife. Suddenly the perfect couple wasn't so perfect. Dr. McDreamy had lied to Meredith, a whopper with enormous repercussions. The audience hated Addison and blamed her for breaking up their dream couple. But even if Addison hadn't arrived on the scene, the contrite wife who wanted her husband back, would Meredith and Derek have survived?

I find this an interesting question and I don't think the answer is as simple as it may have seemed during season one, when Derek and Meredith were the couple everyone wanted them to be. The reason ties into my favorite part of writing and of life: character.

Television drama aside, because of course *Grey's Anatomy* is a TV show that must have conflict in order to bring viewers back each week, what is inherent in Meredith and Derek's characters? What kind of people are they? Are they people capable of monogamous, committed relationships? And if they are, does that automatically mean that *they* would have made it in a world with a high divorce rate and the intense pressures of their respective careers? Not to mention their different status levels at the hospital where they both work.

Let's start with everyone's favorite, Dr. McDreamy. Dr. Derek Shepherd is sexy. He's God's gift to women. Certainly the females he comes into contact with at the hospital would agree. He is an egotist: arrogant, even conceited. He'd have to be in order to be a top-notch neurosurgeon who operates on people's brains every day, taking their lives and their futures into his talented hands.

Derek is also a man capable of compartmentalizing his life. A wife back East. A lover in Seattle. Yet just what was the status of his marriage in his mind when he moved to Seattle and met Meredith Grey? How would he have dealt with the marriage issue had Addison not returned? Would he have divorced his wife? And when would he have told Meredith? Clearly, the longer he waited, the angrier Meredith (or any woman) would be. A lie of this magnitude is poison to any relationship, and yet this never seemed to bother or dawn on him in any way.

Derek is a solitary individual, not given to opening up his trailer, let alone his heart or his emotions. Whether or not his wife returned, she existed, and he never mentioned her. Someone unwilling or unable to communicate the most important facts and feelings in his or her life is a risky long-term bet. Especially for a woman who needs security and stability more than she needs oxygen to breathe.

In fact, even the *Grey's Anatomy* writers point out in their blog on "Save Me" (1-8) that for the first week Meredith was with Derek, she knew nothing about him, his family, what he enjoyed or didn't. She only knew she liked him and that he made her feel good. Needy by nature, Meredith did realize she wasn't privy to important areas of Derek's life and called him on it, but he had the charming ability to turn the subject away until *he* was ready. It is worth noting here that Meredith's neediness (a subject we'll tackle in more depth later) paired with Derek's ability to compartmentalize, and omit select things about himself and his past, can be a particularly bad combination. But for now, back to the beginning.

Eventually Derek showed Meredith his trailer, his land, and his home. And eventually he opened up:

> MEREDITH: Where are we?
> DEREK: Shut up. My mother's maiden name is Maloney. I have four sisters, eight nieces, and five nephews. I like coffee ice cream, single malt Scotch, and occasionally a good cigar. I fly fish, I cheat when I do the Sunday crossword puzzle, and I don't dance in public. My favorite color is blue. And not that light blue. Indigo. *The Sun Also Rises?* Favorite novel. The Clash? Favorite band. This tiny little scar by my nose? That's why I don't ride motorcycles anymore. And I live in that trailer! And all this land is mine and I have no idea what I'm gonna do with it!! That's it, that's all you've earned. For now. The rest . . . well, the rest you'll have to take on faith. ("Save Me," 1-8)

13

Meredith took Derek's word. On faith, she allowed herself to trust. But as the writers reminded us in that same blog entry on "Save Me," "the rest" that Derek asked Meredith to take on faith was his wife. *His wife*: "Not only did Derek not tell Meredith about Addison, he told her everything except that. And then he asked her to have faith in him." The nerve of the man.

When the audience watched that scene for the first time, it seemed pure and simple, honest and beautiful. But when they saw the same segment again in reruns, after they knew about Derek's wife, the scene was painful to watch. Again the writers wondered, *How can Meredith trust Derek after that?*

Good question.

Still, Derek is obviously someone who can make a commitment, which is more than we can say for many men. He took his wife back after she cheated on him. He tried to make his marriage work because, as he reiterated on many occasions, he took vows. And from the moment they reunited, he was loyal to his wife and those vows—or at least tried to be—until he cheated with Meredith at the end of season two. In order to further the argument in favor of Derek and Meredith lasting as a couple based on *his* character, let's assume that he is loyal when invested with one person only. Once he commits and is committed to in return, he doesn't stray. Furthermore, if we do not view Meredith as a woman with whom he violated those marriage vows because Addison betrayed him first—if he truly was in love with Meredith as he has said—then we can draw the conclusion here that Derek is capable of a monogamous long-term commitment.

Yet this isn't the whole story. I find myself looking forward, to the Derek who had to choose between Meredith and his wife. Each time there was a choice to be made, we were led to believe by the writers and by Derek that it was Meredith who had to make it. The finale of season two was a primary example. *Whom would she choose?* But the truth was, Derek expected Meredith to pick between himself and another man when—and to me this is key to Derek's character—*Derek had not yet left his wife.*

So I see Derek as a flawed man who claims to be in love with Meredith, but who made Meredith suffer emotionally by having to watch him with another woman, even though he had never really let her go. An egotist. A man more concerned with his wants and needs than the woman he claims to love. A man who had been emotionally vacant with his first wife. And a man whose attitude and behavior led her to find comfort in the arms of his best friend. Would Derek eventually have done the same to Meredith?

An argument in Derek's favor is that his proximity to Meredith, by virtue of them working in the same hospital and seeing one another every day, would have strengthened the bond between them. However, working in the same hospital didn't save Derek's first marriage. Would proximity have helped Derek and Meredith fare any better?

This leads to Meredith. Even if we were to assume based on Derek's loyalty, which is an admirable character trait, that he would have stayed with Meredith, would she have been on the same page? Is Dr. Meredith Grey capable of sustaining a committed relationship with Derek? Meredith is even more interesting as a character if for no other reason than we have deep insight into her family history. Before we touch on her past, though, let's deal with who she is now.

Dr. Grey is also an egotist, perhaps even more so than Derek. Look at the pain she caused her best friend George. How many times did the poor man try to ask her on a date or tell her he was in love with her only to be tuned out or come second to Meredith's own needs or concerns? She is self-absorbed to the point of extreme arrogance. And yet, she is so human, so flawed, so touching, you can't help but adore her. Clearly Dr. McDreamy feels the same way.

But is love or caring enough? Or will Meredith's neediness, which pervades all aspects of her life, sabotage this relationship, too?

How did Meredith and Derek meet? At a bar. He was a one-night stand for Meredith—one of many in her life. Meredith is the self-proclaimed queen of the one-night stand, which by its nature is exciting (one would hope) and somewhat illicit. The people who partake are drawn together by the thrill of doing something for just one night and not having to deal with the repercussions afterward. To have a future, Meredith must face the after. Would she still have wanted to be with Derek when the newness and excitement of the affair wore off? Or would she have returned to old habits of "picking up strange boys"?

15

If Derek upset her, or ignored her, or tuned her out in favor of work, something which we established seems likely, how long would it have been before she found comfort elsewhere? Not too long, judging by her own admission that her answer to pain or emotional turmoil is an impulsive sexual liaison. Or would her love for Derek have helped Meredith to grow up and find a more adult solution to her problems? Certainly the fact that in her neediness she slept with her best friend, who is so clearly in love with her it's painful to watch, doesn't provide a convincing hope that she's learned from her mistakes.

Often looking to the source of a particular behavior helps a person to understand and perhaps get beyond it. Meredith's neediness has a firm basis in her past. Meredith was raised by a mother who was selfish in the extreme. She cheated on her husband and even flaunted the affair. She belittled her husband's decision to stay with her and ignore her cheating. From this and from Meredith's visit with her estranged father in the middle of season two, we know that he was and is a weak man, who allowed himself to be dominated by his controlling, stronger wife. He wasn't in his daughter's life as a male role model or influence of any kind.

As a result, Meredith has no positive relationship examples to look to or emulate in conducting her own. She has no parent who she feels loved her or validated her worth as a child and those feelings have continued into adulthood. The fact that she has unresolved issues with both parents tells us that she has not found closure there, and so she brings her pain and neediness with her into her relationships.

Like Derek, she doesn't deal with her issues; she runs away from them. He ran to Seattle in order to get away from the fact that his wife cheated on him instead of staying either to fight for her or divorce her. But since her return he has been forced to face his past. Similarly, Meredith is now forced to care for her ailing mother, but she knows she can never resolve their issues, if for no other reason than because her mother's Alzheimer's would prevent any coherent discussion. And just what kind of discussion could Meredith have with the woman who told her she didn't have what it took to cut it as a surgeon? Meredith's relationships with her parents and her unresolved issues are not good indicators of her future ability to sustain a loving relationship.

There are also external factors to consider, particularly their work. Thanks to her mother's profession as a surgeon, Meredith knows the commitment it takes to be married to one. And Meredith is a woman who has aspirations of her own (although she has a long way to go before she reaches Derek's level, career-wise). The fact that Meredith possesses both her own drive and the understanding needed by a surgeon's wife bodes well for them as a couple.

But there would have been roadblocks here, as well. Love in the workplace provides a serious external conflict, one that can be an inconvenience at best or a career-ending issue at worst. Meredith and Derek are not the only ones engaged in an affair that violates hospital policy and good career sense, of course. Seattle Grace is a hotbed of illicit love. So given the other complicated relationships at Seattle Grace, one might wonder: Is it really risky for Meredith and Derek to be together at work? The answer is yes.

They work at a hospital where he is her superior and relationships such as theirs are frowned upon, especially by Meredith's boss at the hospital, Dr. Miranda Bailey, and nobody wants to get on the bad side of "the Nazi." If Meredith could have survived Dr. Bailey's being harder on her because of her relationship with Derek, she would have been a better surgeon in the end, but could she have coped with the added pressure in light of her existing insecurities? Could she have prevented hospital problems from affecting her relationship with Derek? In the past, when Meredith has had problems, her relationships have tended to suffer.

And when dealing with a hospital romance, those problems promise to be big ones. For one thing, the young doctors at Seattle Grace are competing with one another for opportunities. When the others found out about Meredith's relationship with Derek in season one, they assumed she would be given special favors by him: the opportunity to scrub in on surgery, the chance to work on an exciting diagnosis. Squabbling and problems within the group raised difficulties in the hospital, a place already fraught with tension. These tensions would have only increased as the stakes grew higher. What if some doctors were cut from the program, leaving them to wonder if Meredith remained only because of her relationship with Derek?

Would either of them have been strong enough to handle the controversy without damaging their relationship in the process? Derek probably would have been, but let's face it, he would have had less at stake. His career is firmly established. Meredith's career is just beginning.

What if during one of these times, Derek wasn't there for her emotionally? Would Meredith have slept with someone else, as she has in the past? One thing is for sure: It's doubtful Derek would forgive this kind of betrayal a second time.

So far we have painted a bleak future for our favorite couple. Yet despite all the reasons for Meredith and Derek not to work out, there is one shining ray of hope. Ironically, we now return to Addison. The person who tore Meredith and Derek apart might be the thing that allows them to remain together. When Derek's wife showed up, she blew Meredith and Derek's relationship to smithereens. She also exposed their mistakes and their frailties. She gave them time to think, to live, and to learn.

While Derek was trying to make his marriage work, Meredith found a stable man who truly seemed to care about her. However, she also discovered that no matter how good the new relationship seemed to be, her heart belonged to Derek. She discovered (we hope) that turning to other men to fill the emptiness and neediness inside her isn't a successful solution to her problems. She was able to view her mother's past affair and see how it devastated her marriage and her daughter, and also make a kind of peace with her mother regarding it.

During this time, Derek also grew up. He has faced his part in pushing Addison away and the dissolution of his marriage. He knows now that he emotionally abandoned his wife and he (hopefully) understands that just being married isn't enough to secure a future. Successful relationships take work. Commitment is a job outside of both Derek's and Meredith's careers at the hospital. Part of that work includes truth and candor. If Addison hadn't shown up, Derek wouldn't have learned this powerful lesson.

With luck, Addison's return has taught both Meredith and Derek the power of forgiveness for both minor indiscretions as well as major ones. Because only if they grow both as individuals as well as a couple, and only if they love each other enough to learn from past mistakes, will they stand a chance at a future. Derek must continue to open himself up more, while Meredith must look inward for strength instead of blindly hoping to find it in a stranger's arms.

18

———

Postscript: When I first wrote this essay at the beginning of season three, it continued, "The fact is that Meredith and Derek are a television couple, and happiness equals death on a televised serial. After all, how long can viewers watch them sip drinks outside Derek's trailer before they grow bored? How long then until the lack of conflict convinces the writers of the need to drive Derek and Meredith apart?" The answer, of course, turned out to be "the end of season three." Conflict between the two was always guaranteed. Yet television is a business and as such, it is driven by the need to satisfy its viewers. If so, if the "customer is always right" theory applies, then *Grey's Anatomy's* favorite couple, Derek and Meredith, must end up together. The viewers demand it.

I, for one, will root for Meredith and Derek because of the longing they so clearly feel for one another in such a soul-deep way, and I will trust that the past and the present will sustain them in the future—no matter how often Meredith lives down to expectations and Derek gives up rather than fights for what he wants. And because this is television, I hope that when the dust settles and the series ends, Meredith and Derek will end up together after all.

Happily ever after—in our minds and our hearts, forever.

Does any place else really matter?

CARLY PHILLIPS started her writing career with Harlequin Temptation in 1999 with Brazen, and she's never strayed far from home! Carly has since published twenty-five books, including the *New York Times* bestsellers *The Bachelor, Summer Lovin'*, and *Hot Item*. An avid TV watcher and *Grey's Anatomy* lover, Carly lives in Purchase, New York, with her husband, two daughters, and a frisky soft-coated wheaten terrier who acts like their third child. Contact Carly at: P.O. Box 483, Purchase, NY 10577, or visit her cyber home at www.carlyphillips.com.

Imagine the cast of *Grey's Anatomy* as wolves. No, seriously—give it a shot. Elizabeth Engstrom did, and came up with some compelling conclusions about inter-intern relations, Burke and Cristina, and the perils of dating alpha wolves.

Elizabeth Engstrom

WHY DRS. GREY AND SHEPHERD WILL NEVER LIVE HAPPILY EVER AFTER

Sleeping with the boss is never a good idea.

Some call it "fouling your own nest," perhaps for good reason. Others call it fraternization, realizing the potential for sexual harassment problems among those of unequal power. Some companies have strict policies against it; others seem to understand that the workplace is the center of most employees' social lives, and it's only natural that, as mammals, we will breed with those in proximity. Whatever the situation, whatever the policy, a love affair gone wrong among coworkers makes for too much drama in the workplace, and most businesses don't like it.

But viewers love it.

The writers of *Grey's Anatomy* have taken this an extra step, giving us two contrasting sets of workplace romances: Dr. Meredith Grey with Dr. Derek Shepherd, and Dr. Cristina Yang with Dr. Preston Burke. Yang and Burke have a chance of making it, but Drs. Grey and Shepherd? Not a prayer.

———

Men Are from Mars, Women Are from Venus author Dr. John Gray made the general public aware, back in the 1980s, of the multitudinous differences between men and women. Since then, countless studies have proven his points with regards to the way we think, act, and relate, from the physical aspects of the brain (women have an actual physiological aptitude for multi-tasking and perhaps even intuiting) all the way down to primitive mating rituals (over which we seem to be relatively helpless).

Men and women approach everything differently, but we are total opposites when it comes to falling in love. Consider this: Men tend to fall in love with women they are attracted to, and women become attracted to the men they've fallen in love with.

Could anything be more opposite?

For example: In order for a man to want to get to know a woman, he must first be attracted to her. Once attracted, he will make a move.

Burke brought Cristina a coffee.

A woman, on the other hand, can *suddenly* become attracted to an old family friend, or someone she's known socially for years: her husband's brother, her husband's best friend, her brother's best friend, her son's best friend (God forbid), her neighbor, her co-worker. Over time, she has come to know him, she has fallen in love with him, and sexual attraction has followed on love's heels.

Cristina drank the coffee and couldn't stop thinking about it.

If you want to see the mating dance at its most primitive, go to the mall. The girls—makeup perfect, clothes perfect, hair perfect—are seeking the attentions of a "nice" guy. The boys, slovenly and cool, slouch around looking for a "hot" girl. She's looking for values; he's looking to broadcast his seed. She wants to marry the captain of the football team; he wants to fuck the head cheerleader.

That first night when Meredith met Derek, she looked hot, and he was attracted.

She was just looking for some touch. Then she got to know him, as he relentlessly pursued her. When she finally agreed to actually date him, her affections were rising. She'd gotten to know him, was falling in love, and his sexual appeal was growing. She could no longer refuse his requests for a little extracurricular dalliance.

By the time she agreed to go out, of course, he was already smitten. First, he was attracted to her, and then he got to know her, and his attraction grew. Finally, it ripened into whatever kind of love a man can have that lets him say, "Oh, Meredith, I'm so sorry," as his never-before-

22

revealed wife walks through the door ("Who's Zoomin' Who?," 1-9).

To recap: She's hot, he's nice. She's looking for values (at least after that first night); he's looking to hook up and gets caught in love's snare.

And what of Burke and Cristina?

She's hot; he's attracted. He's nice; she's attracted. He pursued her until she caught him.

Textbook.

And yet, while these couples share much in common, there's one big difference between them: their respective statuses within their social orders—within their packs. And that difference has everything to do with whether their relationships will succeed.

———

Humans are not dogs, but we engage in pack behavior more often than we like to admit. Mob mentality is a kind of pack behavior. The military hierarchy depends upon pack mentality to keep everyone in line. But for a moment, let's talk about wolves. See if you see any similarities between the typical pack of wolves and the activities at Seattle Grace Hospital— or your office, your family, or any social group to which you belong.

Wolves are extremely sociable and highly intelligent animals. They typically live in packs of five to ten, and function as a cooperative family unit. Pack animal behavior is instinctive. Every pack has a hierarchy, and every animal in the pack has duties, responsibilities, and expectations.

In every pack there is an alpha. The alpha and his/her mate comprise the alpha pair. The alpha leads the pack and makes important decisions concerning the welfare of the group. Just below the alpha pair is the beta wolf, then the subordinates. At the bottom of the hierarchy is the omega wolf. This wolf is the scapegoat and will bear the brunt of the pack's frustrations and harassment. It will usually be the last to feed, and will go without if food is scarce.

Any of this seem familiar?

It's all about power.

———

The *Grey's Anatomy* cast falls into two specific packs: the surgical interns and the hospital staff.

Of the surgical interns, George O'Malley is the omega. He is much-maligned and disrespected, simply because he seems to have been born to it. Even his family treats him with disdain: Witness the ridiculous family turkey hunt, or the way his brothers took anyone's opinion over George's at the hospital when their father was admitted. George has no power, and he knows it.

The hospital staff's omega, on the other hand, is the person who, logically, ought to have the most power: Dr. Richard Webber, Chief of Surgery. He, like George O'Malley, is a tragic figure. He has regularly had to remind the other doctors that he is the Chief, and when he's down, the other residents counsel him. He's even more likely to eat at the lunch table with the surgical interns than with his peers.

Cristina Yang, Izzie Stevens, and Alex Karev are in the middle of the surgical interns' pack. They contribute to the welfare of the group, and acknowledge their alpha's leadership, but otherwise carry on with their lives. Similarly, the middle of the hospital staff pack is comprised of Preston Burke, Miranda Bailey, Addison Montgomery-Shepherd, Mark Sloan, and Callie Torres.

24

Which leaves us with our alphas: Meredith Grey and Derek Shepherd.

———

There is no doubt that Dr. Meredith Grey is the pack leader of the surgical interns. When something stressful happens to her, the pack gathers around. When Meredith bravely held onto the bomb and narrowly escaped being blown to bits, Izzie and Cristina even got into the shower with her, to help her clean up and to comfort her. But when something stressful happens to Izzie, George, Alex, or Cristina, the others generally expect him or her to just get over it. Witness, for example, the way Meredith and Izzie viewed George's relationship troubles with Callie: callously, actually, which added to George's stress.

Meredith's head emerges above the fray not only because she is the star of the show, but because she is not blind with ambition. She is young but secure, confident in her choices (even when they prove not to be in her best interest), and shows leadership as landlady, confidante, and best friend to the members of her pack.

Dr. Derek Shepherd is just as clearly the alpha of the hospital. He exhibits all the alpha qualities: quiet confidence, dignity, intelligence, and an air of authority. Nobody questions Dr. Shepherd. People sometimes advise him, but no one tells him what to do.

Alpha is an attitude. Alphas stand tall and use their voices and eyes to project the idea that they're capable of getting what they want. They're gentle but firm, loving but tough, all at the same time. Non-alphas are immediately submissive toward alphas because they recognize and respect this type of power when they see it.

Alphas get the best of everything. The best food, the best place to sleep, the best patients. And Dr. Shepherd got to sleep with Dr. Grey. At least he did, for a while, until Addison re-entered the picture—and even then, he got to watch Meredith yearn for him. (And chances are, he will again.)

There's another alpha trait that both Meredith and Derek exhibit, and that is the "alpha stare."

It's not a challenge, or at least it doesn't have to be. It is an unafraid, eye-to-eye, confident gaze that either comforts or intimidates, depending on the frame of mind of the receiver.

George looks down a lot, coupled with furtive glances. Cristina's eyes dart back and forth as if she's searching for something—validation perhaps. But Meredith boldly looks ahead. She, in all her wounded misery, still looked Shepherd square in the eye. She never once backed down. She was unrepentant for her feelings, for her hopes and dreams. She was unapologetic for her broken heart, and placed the lion's share of the blame directly upon him.

He took that gaze and threw it right back to her. I can't remember ever seeing a character who had so mastered the sorrowful look of sincere empathy for a person in pain, when he himself was the genesis of that pain. His looks of concern and regret—without apology—were at once endearing and infuriating.

Grey to Shepherd in "Raindrops Keep Falling on My Head" (2-1): "What was I to you? The girl you screwed to get over being screwed?"

He responded: "You were like coming up for fresh air. It's like I was drowning and you saved me. It's all I know."

Grey: "It's not enough."

Classic alpha dialogue. Crisp, to the point, nobody even flinched.

———

An interesting sideline to this examination is Dr. Shepherd's relationship with Dr. Burke.

Shepherd's alpha status interfered with his friendship with Burke, in that Burke was on a first-name basis with all his peers, but did not allow Shepherd the same courtesy: a petty little power play.

That didn't really bother Shepherd. He merely found it curious.

Then, when Shepherd showed his courage under fire and gained Burke's respect, he was allowed first-name status.

But what's interesting here is that Burke was disrespecting Shepherd for doing dirt to Meredith, yet Burke's respect was regained because of Shepherd's courage in seeing to his patient while a bomb was threatening his operating room.

Burke was mixing apples and oranges here—unless you're considering the power the alpha has over the rest of the pack. Burke, as a subordinate, resented the way Shepherd got away with sexual shenanigans, yet he wanted to be a loyal member. As soon as Shepherd gave him an excuse, he re-committed to his underling status, acknowledging Shepherd's alpha status, and equilibrium was restored.

None of it mattered, one way or the other, to the alpha.

26

———

While Meredith didn't know that Derek was going to be her boss when she picked him up in a bar and took him home that first night, it isn't surprising that they chose each other. Head cheerleaders always want to breed with the captain of the football team. It's a classic survival of the fittest instinct. Little girls all have crushes on their daddies, secretaries sleep with their bosses, nurses have affairs with the doctors, flight attendants flirt with airline captains, students fall in lust with their teachers. We all want to mate with the alpha dog.

The problem here is that *both* Meredith and Derek have alpha status, in separate packs. And that makes them incompatible. Their social responsibilities (leading their subordinates, seeing to the well-being of their group) conflict, if for no other reason than because their packs are in constant conflict. In many instances—the whole Denny Duquette debacle, for example—the two packs work at cross purposes. In addition to their personal relationship matters, not an insignificant element when one is sleeping with one's boss, they have their pack status to protect and defend. And neither Derek nor Meredith can switch packs to become half of the other's alpha pair: Meredith could not possibly be an alpha at the hospital, and Derek would never be allowed as alpha of the surgical interns. Their relationship, inevitably, is doomed.

Dr. Yang and Dr. Burke's relationship, though unbalanced because she's an intern and he's a surgeon, is nevertheless more stable. Both hold the beta positions in their respective packs. And they're both good, healthy members of those packs—they contribute to the welfare of the whole, discipline peers, and accept being disciplined. Neither one takes control, dominates, or in any other way exhibits any alpha characteristics. I would say that the long-term prognosis for this quirky couple is good, except that this is television, and television is all about drama and conflict.

Stay tuned.

————

As more is revealed in subsequent seasons, I will be interested to watch how the two separate-yet-inextricably-linked power dynamics—Grey and Shepherd, Yang and Burke—evolve.

These characters are not wolves, despite all evidence to the contrary. They are complex human beings with intricate emotional needs, and they have brilliant writers giving them voice.

And, of course, the reason this type of drama—whether on film, television, or in a book—is so popular is that we like to dive inside the characters, try on their clothes, and see if we would act the way they act, were we magically thrown into their situation.

We learn things about ourselves in the process.

There's one thing I've learned from watching this series, and I hope you have, too. It's this:

Alpha or not, unless you want this type of drama in your life, sleeping with the boss is never a good idea.

ELIZABETH ENGSTROM is the author of nine books and more than 250 short stories, articles, and essays. She teaches the fine art of fiction at writers conferences and conventions around the world, and is currently a regular contributor to Court TV's *Crime Library*. You can visit her Web site at www.elizabethengstrom.com.

In the halls of Seattle Grace, Beth Kendrick has noticed, motherhood means something a little different. Pregnant surgical interns get transferred to the "vagina squad" (as Cristina put it in "Raindrops Keep Falling on My Head" [2-1]); female surgeons with kids get "mommy-tracked." All in all, *Grey's Anatomy* doesn't make having a baby seem particularly appealing. The question is—why?

Beth Kendrick

"WE DON'T DO WELL WITH MOTHERS HERE"

THE PERILS OF PARENTING AT SEATTLE GRACE

Here are the three commandments of becoming a surgeon, according to a recent med school grad:

1. No lying, no crying.
2. Eat and sleep whenever you get the chance.
3. Don't mess with the pancreas.

But there appears to be a fourth cardinal rule at work in Seattle Grace Hospital:

4. Motherhood and surgery don't mix.

You don't mess with the pancreas because it's basically a big, mysterious bag of digestive enzymes—an extremely delicate, temperamental organ that affects the surrounding systems in unpredictable ways. And you don't swap your scrubs for a maternity dress for the same reason—becoming a mother sets off a chain reaction through the psyche and heart that irrevocably changes the way you practice medicine. A good

29

surgery is clean, precise, and free of complications. A good mother-child relationship is exactly the opposite.

In the surgical wing of Seattle Grace, mothers, by definition, are patients—passive and in distress. Pregnancy is presented as a medical problem to be solved, a crisis to be averted, a mire of complications. For a surgeon to save others' pregnancies, she can't possibly have a family of her own. Her life must always come second to her job. Motherhood is a distraction, and distractions make for sloppy surgeries.

ELLIS GREY: WORST MOTHER, BEST SURGEON

Dr. Ellis Grey had no illusions about the choice she had to make when she had a baby. Everyone, from Meredith's father to Liz the scrub nurse, is matter-of-fact about Ellis's superlative skills as a surgeon and spectacular failings as a mom. Ellis knows she is generally regarded as a ball-busting bitch, and is proud of this reputation. It means she is respected by her male peers. It means she doesn't let emotions get in the way of good medicine. It also means that her daughter grew up essentially without a mother, raised by . . . well, we don't know who raised Meredith, actually, given that her father left in her early childhood. Viewers know Ellis only as well as Meredith knows her, which is to say not at all. Ellis reveals the occasional tantalizing tidbit of her life story through the fog of Alzheimer's, but for the most part, we are left to fill in the blanks ourselves. It's too late for Meredith to forge a real relationship with her mother—all she can do now is assume the role of caretaker and try to move forward into adulthood without parents, siblings, or any extended familial support network.

Given Ellis's passion for her work, we have to assume that Meredith's conception was accidental, and that her role in her mother's life was primarily that of dead weight. Meredith is well aware that her mother resents her: "How many times have I told you not to bother me at work?" Ellis screamed when she was admitted to Seattle Grace and spied her daughter in the corridor ("Make Me Lose Control," 2-3). The rage with which Ellis said this told us everything we need to know about the frustration (and, perhaps, the shame) she feels about her failings as a parent. Self-righteous arrogance was her only defense against "mommy guilt"—her patients needed her more than her child did. End of story.

As an adult, Meredith still craves her mother's approval. She saw what Ellis's career did to her family, yet she decided to become a surgeon against her mother's advice. Surgery is the only real connection Meredith has with Ellis, and it is significant that she chose to do her internship in the hospital that was her mother's home base.

Becoming a surgeon is Meredith's way of rebelling against her mother while simultaneously demanding her respect (surgical skill is the only currency that has any value with Ellis) and feeding Meredith's own self-destructive, "dark and twisty" side. Just like her mother, Meredith fell into a forbidden love affair with a co-worker, then retreated to the OR when her emotional life got complicated (like on Thanksgiving.) And when Meredith was forced to assume the role of caretaker to her mother, she behaved just as Ellis did: avoidant, ambivalent, terrified of getting too close. In "Break on Through" (2-15), Meredith panicked that her mother was going to die alone, but that is the nature of a female surgeon: to aggressively isolate herself. Emotional distance, after all, is the key to success when you're about to slice someone open and literally touch their heart.

31

CRISTINA YANG: CONTROL FREAK OUT OF CONTROL

Cristina is a fascinating study in contradictions: she knows everything about the brain and nothing about psychology, she's a lifelong rule-follower who suddenly starts an illicit affair with her boss, she's an anal-retentive perfectionist whose personal living space is the definition of chaos. She's brilliant, she's fearless, and she makes sure everyone knows it. She's on track to be the next Ellis Grey.

There's just one little catch: Cristina can't take care of herself.

When Burke asked her to move in with him, Cristina offered up her squalid wreck of a luxury apartment as proof that she's unfit to live with another human being. Every time she opens her locker at the hospital, it's crammed full of everything from exotic lingerie to empty candy wrappers. She looks great on the outside, but she's a mess on the inside, and she knows it. This is why she keeps pushing Burke away—she doesn't want him to see how apprehensive and vulnerable and (let's face it) selfish she can be. Sharing her body with Burke is fun and easy, but every time she's pushed to bare her heart and soul, she freezes and/or pulls back and/or goes in search of hard liquor. She defines herself solely by academic accomplishments, which protects her from having to examine her intrinsic sense of self-worth.

Cristina got pregnant despite her best efforts at birth control. This shook her to her core not only because she was completely opposed to having a child, but because the pregnancy proved that, no matter what the medical textbooks say, the body sometimes triumphs over the mind. Science is Cristina's Holy Grail. She wanted to believe that modern medicine is infallible, but two little pink lines proved that nature can find ways around science.

At first, Cristina faced the unplanned pregnancy the way she does every other adversary—with direct action and without emotion. She scheduled an abortion around her surgical rotation schedule and froze out the clinic administrator's well-meaning attempts at counseling. Like Ellis Grey, she works through her problems in stoic isolation. She kept the pregnancy secret from Burke and most of her fellow interns; she had to, because the embryo growing inside her was evidence that she was secretly out of control. She kept up the good front and soldiered on through morning sickness and fatigue, but she couldn't power through the psychological implications so easily. Cristina didn't frame abortion in terms of moral absolutes—that would go against her value system—but she was deeply distressed nonetheless. She couldn't allow herself to even consider carrying the baby to term because she was terrified by the black hole of neediness that an infant represents.

"You know what happens to pregnant interns," Cristina said to Meredith. "I am not switching to the vagina squad or spending my life popping zits" ("Raindrops Keep Falling on My Head," 2-1). But even though she dismissed motherhood with typical bravado, the abrupt end to her ectopic pregnancy was what finally brought Cristina to her knees. She collapsed and found herself, for the first time, a helpless patient on the OR table. During the recovery process, we started to see the first cracks in her veneer. She blamed her weakness on Burke ("He turned me into this fat, stupid, pregnant girl who *cares*!" ("Enough is Enough [No More Tears]," 2-2) and on her own mother, whose misguided attempts to comfort her ailing daughter drove Cristina to the brink of matricide.

The end of Cristina's pregnancy forced her to take a long, hard look at her own limitations. Sometimes preparation and sheer force of will just aren't enough. Her body aborted on its own before she had a chance to take control. Not that she accepted this gracefully. Overwhelmed with the unexpected grief that accompanied her miscarriage, Cristina was still turning to medicine to heal her emotional wounds: "*Somebody sedate me!!!*" ("Deny Deny Deny," 2-4).

But it was too late for her to turn back. She can never go back to being the über-rational, ruthless intern she was before the pregnancy. Almost against her will, she started making friends, sharing insight and informa-tion with her competition, and even helped Izzie cover up the details of the LVAD debacle that resulted in Denny Duquette's death. The old Cristina would have turned Izzie in and never looked back. The new Cristina couldn't. That realization drove her to tears again in the season two finale: "I've always been the one with the answers, and now I don't have any. I can't tell you what happened in that room and before, I could have. No guilt, no loyalties, no problems. I wouldn't have gotten involved. . . . I had an edge, and I lost it" ("Losing My Religion," 2-27).

33

Izzie Stevens: Biological Timebomb

Motherhood is a deep, dark secret for Seattle Grace's surgical interns. We saw this with Meredith, who lied about Ellis's location and condition to Dr. Webber and the hospital staff; we saw this with Cristina, who hid her pregnancy from even the baby's father; and we see this with Izzie, who, even though she is the most stereotypically maternal intern (baking cup-cakes, decorating the house for Christmas), keeps her identity as a mother from her closest friends.

Izzie has revealed only to a pregnant sixteen-year-old patient that she had a daughter in high school and gave her up for adoption. "There's more than one way to be a good mother," she said. "I wanted more for her than I could do at sixteen" ("Break on Through," 2-15). But we know she feels the loss deeply—she couldn't talk about her daughter without crying, and she carries a photograph of the child she had to give up. When the patient's mother angrily demanded that Izzie stop talking to her daughter about the benefits of adoption, Izzie replied, "If you can get past the fact that I'm superior and I'm judging you and I'm telling you what's best for your family . . . isn't it possible that I'm also right?" ("Break on Through").

Izzie did the right thing eleven years ago and gave up her daughter. But the sacrifice obviously affected her deeply, and she's refused to give up on anyone else since. She gets overly attached to her patients, a tendency for which she has been repeatedly reprimanded by Dr. Bailey and Dr. Montgomery-Shepherd, and which ultimately proved deadly for Denny.

It's interesting that, given her inability to distance herself from her patients, Izzie dates men who make it impossible for her to get romantically attached. In season one, she was nominally involved in a long-distance relationship with a hockey player who broke up with her when she refused to cut back her work hours. In season two, she started flirting with Alex, who made a point of posturing as a crude, callous, misogynist jerk. She became convinced she could save him—that she alone could coax out the sweet, sensitive Alex no one else could see. But Alex would not be coaxed—instead, he sabotaged the relationship by sleeping with Olivia and "forgetting" to lock the on-call room door. This actually seemed to increase her physical attraction to him, and she initiated a no-strings, friends-with-benefits fling with him once it was clear they couldn't cultivate a deep emotional attachment.

"You only like your men sick and feeble," Denny teased when Izzie suddenly became shy and fluttery after he survived a successful heart transplant. Izzie laughed this off, but the truth is, she does have a deep-seated rescue complex. From a psychological standpoint, one could make the case that every sick preemie, every patient who flatlines, represents the infant she had to surrender. "What about me?" she cried when Denny signs the DNR papers. "You'll be fine [when you're dead and in heaven], but what about me?!?" ("17 Seconds," 2-25).

Fear of letting go and again giving up her beloved is what ultimately renders Izzie unable to do the right thing when it came to Denny. She told herself that she was acting in his best interests, but when she cut the LVAD wire, she was beyond reason. She was crazed, defiant, willing to go to any lengths to avoid what she saw as another unbearable loss. And she did manage to hold on to him, though only for a few more hours. She let emotion supersede medical judgment and ended up losing everything: Denny, her good standing in the internship program, her sense of purpose and self-confidence. Dr. Bailey blamed herself for letting Izzie spin so far out of control: "I went soft. I had a baby and I swore it wouldn't change me, but it does change you. . . . I went soft" ("I Am a Tree," 3-2).

MIRANDA BAILEY: NAZI NO MORE

None of the female surgical interns have a good relationship with their own mothers; Miranda Bailey is the closest thing they have to a maternal role model. And she sets a fine example of a surgeon—tough on herself but always considerate of her patients. Good is not good enough for Bailey; she's always striving for better. She bosses around the attending physicians and the Chief. She is "the Nazi."

Or she was, until she got mommy-tracked.

"When you operate, the rest of the world goes away. Hunger, thirst, pain: you don't feel it in the OR. But it's not that way when you're sharing your body with another person" ("Grandma Got Run Over by a Reindeer," 2-12). And it wasn't that way after the baby was born. Being a mother changes a surgeon, but perhaps more importantly, it changes other people's perceptions of that surgeon. "I have not gone soft" became Bailey's refrain in season two, until finally, in season three, she admitted that she had.

Miranda, like Cristina, saw "going soft" not as gaining a sense of empathy, but as losing her edge. On the plane ride to a transplant site, Bailey confessed to Cristina that she, too, had considered terminating her pregnancy. After much deliberation, she had decided that "I knew I could do this. . . . You just have to know. You do what you can, while you can" ("Grandma Got Run Over by a Reindeer"). But as the only female intern in her class who clawed her way up the ranks against the odds, Bailey doesn't give up control without a struggle. When she went into labor, she first determined that the baby would be born on a schedule, and then, when she discovered that her husband had been in a car accident and wouldn't make it to the delivery room, she decided to pack up, go home, and give birth another day. She was willing to endanger her health and that of her baby rather than surrender her all-encompassing urge to maintain control.

Bailey also didn't do well with the whole "maternity leave" thing. She returned to work ahead of schedule, ready to prove that she still had what it took, only to find that her name was mysteriously absent from the OR board. Dr. Webber insisted that he was not discriminating against her, but Bailey knew better: "I'm covered in mommy. But that does not mean I will be mommy-tracked" ("The Name of the Game," 2-22). She convinced Dr. Shepherd to let her assist on a brain operation of a young boy. For the first time, we saw Bailey openly show emotion about a patient—she actually wept with relief when Dr. Shepherd saved him. This did not make her any less skilled as a surgeon, but it did affect her colleagues' perception of her.

Finally, the Chief admitted he was going to be treating her differently: "I'm not convinced you're back on your game. This is not a punishment or a reflection of how highly I value you. It's just the way it is" ("Blues for Sister Someone," 2-23). Indeed, many of Bailey's male peers view her maternal state as an intractable weakness; during the hospital inquest of Denny's death, she was directly accused by a fellow physician: "Sleep deprivation coupled with wild swings in hormones are factors that could cloud anyone's judgment. . . . [Denny] died due to [your] poor decision making" ("Oh, the Guilt," 3-5).

36

In an attempt to prove that she was still the Nazi, Bailey forced herself to be callous and dismissive of a patient's husband and infant son because she didn't want to be seen as the "baby whisperer." Dr. Webber took her aside and advised her not to give in to the peer pressure to be constantly, disdainfully aloof: "Compassion and empathy are a big part of [this] job. . . . Being a parent makes you a better doctor" ("Oh, the Guilt"). Easy for him to say—he has no children, attended family functions only when threatened with divorce, and eventually split from his wife when she forced him to choose between his marriage and his surgical career. Dr. Bailey knows the truth, and shared it with a female patient facing a mastectomy in "Oh, the Guilt": To be a great mother is to be human and to feel overwhelmed by the full range of human emotions, and you can't just turn that off when you pick up a scalpel.

———

Grey's Anatomy is different from most other medical dramas in that it was created by a woman, is written mostly by women, and focuses primarily on female characters. So at first glance, it seems surprising that the show would portray motherhood as, essentially, an impediment.

But maybe the writers aren't being negative; maybe they're just being honest. Unlike men, women don't have the luxury of ignoring the realities of parenthood. The unpopular and unsettling truth is, being a mother *is* exhausting, it *does* affect your job performance, and it *will* change who you are at your very core. After devoting decades of her life to school and grueling professional preparation, no one can blame a female surgeon for looking beyond the "having it all" myth. She can't afford to delude herself; the stakes are too high. Refer to the first rule of surgery, "no lying, no crying" . . . and parent at your own risk.

As the owner of three wild and crazy dogs, BETH KENDRICK was a big fan of McVet (Finn, we hardly knew ye!). Her novels include *Nearlyweds, Fashionably Late, Exes and Ohs,* and *My Favorite Mistake.* You can visit her Web site at www.bethkendrick.com.

The women get a lot of credit in *Grey's Anatomy*, as far as defying stereotypes goes—as well they should. They're a diverse (and I don't mean ethnically, though that's true as well) group of strong, flawed women: from obnoxiously ambitious Cristina to insecure, dark-and-twisty Meredith; from stiff, proud Ellis to sharp-tongued, soft-hearted Bailey. But amidst all that feminist boundary-pushing, it's easy to miss the men—and, as Todd Gilchrist suggests, *Grey's Anatomy's* male counterparts are just as revolutionary.

Todd Gilchrist

GREY'S ANATOMY AND THE NEW MAN

One of the great virtues of episodic television—and long-form storytelling in general—is the opportunity for the audience to really get to know the characters. Movies, unless they're ten-hour experimental epics or spectacle-laden trilogies, seldom if ever render characters in terms that allow for much complexity. This proves especially true with male characters, who time and again are called upon to contribute strength, humor, or dramatic adversity for the other characters, usually without explanation or real rationale. But on the small screen, across a season or two of terrific television? Everything should, can, and will be explained, whether it's that nasty competitive edge, that comic defense mechanism, or that irresistible charm, manifested years ago when they realized that their wife/girlfriend/mother could never love them as much as they needed.

Historically, leading men on TV dramas have been cut mostly from one cloth: rugged alpha males who tackle tough issues at work but leave the *feelings* for their lady friends. These are guys in whose hands audiences feel safe, whether they're saving lives, solving cases, or shooting bad guys, and who largely dominate their romantic relationships. Moreover, these men are filtered through a particularly narrow prism of moral and ethical correctness, notwithstanding the bedside manner of a few doctors from previous decades, and are regarded as leaders rather than followers.

Recent years have seen a preponderance of increasingly complicated male characters on television. Much of this evolution can be attributed to our collective validation of male feelings—or at the very least, the acknowledgment that males *have* feelings. The mid-nineties in particular produced a real wealth of guys on TV who weren't afraid to show their softer side: Chandler and Ross, for example, provided opposite sides of the same coin on *Friends*, and personified this tenuous evolution of male sensitivity (disguised as rapid-fire wit and tender neuroticism, respectively). Fortunately or unfortunately, such portrayals spawned a backlash from both male and female viewers, who wanted to see, empathize with, or even desire men they felt were genuinely worthy of their admiration.

Subsequently, *Sex and the City* almost literally pitted these two forces against each other, via Mr. Big and Aidan, for the fate of future TV leading men; perhaps unsurprisingly, the classic image of a man—the competitive, sometimes insensitive, quite often incorrigible Big—took home Carrie at the end of the show, leaving countless ladies (and more than a few hopeful men) divided on whether the knight-in-shining-armor should in fact thwart the color-coordinated-conflict-resolution-specialist. But when the show ended in 2004, suffice it to say that audiences were invigorated by the possibilities opened up by the show; what would come next to satiate their need for role models and, more often, regular fantasy objects?

While perhaps not the only or even first post-*Sex* show to explore this same territory, *Grey's Anatomy* takes a similar and at once strikingly different approach in its examination of gender politics. Shonda Rhimes, the show's creator, has envisioned a hospital and by extension a world where men are both strong and sensitive, fierce and fallible—in other words, complicated and complex as the ones in the real world. Featuring a decidedly more expansive cast of characters who often interact in intersecting but not necessarily overlapping social circles, the show's five male leads—Derek Shepherd, Richard Webber, George O'Malley, Alex Karev, and Preston Burke—reveal much not only about the characters

40

themselves, but the kind of men we want them to be and, further, the very way that we look at modern men in general.

Dr. Derek Shepherd

Derek Shepherd is, for all intents and purposes, the Mr. Big of *Grey's Anatomy*. No male character has more visibly enchanted, infuriated, or just plain invigorated a romantic subplot since Mr. Big turned Carrie's world upside down, over and over again, on *Sex and the City*. But is it because of that familiarity that we wonder and watch to see whether he and Meredith, our star-crossed lovers, will come together, or in spite of it? Whichever is your reason, that relationship makes for some spectacularly engaging drama and typifies the fundamental conflict between yesteryear's rugged loverman and today's sensitive romantic lead.

Shepherd was the first male character we actually saw on the show, and he made a decidedly memorable first impression—facedown on the floor, completely bereft of clothing after a one-night stand. His subsequent behavior seemed to follow the "Big" paradigm: Upon discovering that he and Meredith work together, he continued his seduction of the intern, forgoing all thoughts of propriety and professionalism in lieu of the pleasures of the flesh. But almost as soon as the pair found themselves ensconced in a torrid, semi-secret affair, their relationship was interrupted by the news that Shepherd had a wife, and she had arrived in Seattle to reclaim him. While admittedly this was devastating news to Meredith, it perhaps should have come as less of a surprise to viewers, who have seen countless male characters satisfy their physical and emotional desires regardless of their previous commitments.

What was unique about Derek was his sensitivity in the face of such conventional male behavior: While he avoided sharing his checkered past with his wife Addison with Meredith, he did seek to comfort her when she responded negatively to the revelation. In fact, he eventually became frustrated by his inability to make her feel better—produced by no small amount of guilt for having deceived her—which in a way was what sent him back to his wife, whom he has no energy for and little interest in comforting, much less interacting with at all. But as Meredith herself later acknowledged, women don't give up on a guy like Derek,

41

precisely because he is attuned to sense and responds supportively to others' feelings; so even if his efforts in his dealings with Meredith were a byproduct of his own guilt, he channeled them positively into trying to assuage her despair.

Meanwhile, Derek's male competitive spirit manifested itself multiple times during the series in both business and personal spheres, first against Burke, who was his competitor for the Chief of Surgery position, and later against almost anyone who dated or became involved romantically with Meredith. But what this revealed about him, at least in the latter case, was not simply that he was just a "guy" interested in winning at all costs. Rather, it was that his feelings for Meredith ran so deep and had manifested themselves at such a subconscious level that he could not reconcile his own doubts about his marriage to Addison and the undercurrent of certainty that he could make things work with Meredith—if only he could sever his old relationship and move on fully to this new one.

Season two produced a number of conundrums for Meredith and Derek, not the least of which was Meredith's own full confession that she wanted him to leave Addison, pick her instead, and naturally live happily ever after. Their prom-night clinch, born as much out of unresolved sexual tension, internal frustration, and jealousy as genuine passion for one another, may have worsened things all around. The happiness Derek was working toward with Addison was again thrown out of whack, with the further complication that he was no longer Meredith's "friend"—a supportive but objective participant in her personal woes—but instead a guy who kept her hanging on to their mutual detriment.

So what does all this mean? In short, that Derek is a little bit like Mr. Big redefined, or maybe just Big combined with Aidan, which means that audiences don't need to be split on which of her leading men Meredith should end up with. (We don't count Finn, who was a stopgap but hardly the replacement that Meredith needed or audiences wanted.) Derek Shepherd is beholden to his feelings certainly more than his television predecessors, but not so much that he won't indulge his more basic desires—which leaves us with yet another dilemma now that we've actually seen him for what he is: Which "version" of Derek do we want—the loverman or romantic lead?

DR. RICHARD WEBBER

What is it about the Chief of Surgery that inspires such awe, such reverence, such . . . sympathy? On *Grey's Anatomy*, it could be the fact that Dr. Richard Webber is constantly corrected by his subordinates. Or it could be the fact that in the course of two seasons he underwent surgery for a brain tumor and suffered a mild heart attack. Or it could very well be because he is in charge of maintaining order in a hospital populated by ambitious, unruly, contentious physicians, not to mention doing so while projecting a veneer of normalcy and professionalism to the outside world.

During season one, Webber played a decidedly less integral role in the *Grey's* universe, except in the capacity that a Chief did in fact exist, and both Shepherd and Burke were up for his top-dog position if they played their cards right. In fact, all outward evidence suggested that Webber was precisely the kind of Chief that a hospital should have: strong, intelligent, decisive, and unemotional—in short, everything embodied in the "classic" male model. The first example of this was in the season one finale "Who's Zoomin' Who?" (1-9), when he discovered (during surgery, natch) that his vision was faltering. He promptly left the operating room, leaving the surgery to Dr. Bailey, less because of fear of humiliation than his appreciation for the responsibilities of a surgeon. In a medical environment, personal pride must take a backseat to professionalism, and Webber knew that he must remove himself from the situation if for no other reason than the fact that a person's life was literally at stake.

That said, however, Webber was certainly not above strategically hiding his weakness (real or perceived) from the rest of the hospital staff, which can be attributed to his masculine hubris as much as to the necessity of maintaining a strong, authoritative chain of command. His first decision after realizing that his vision was impaired was to contact Dr. Shepherd, the facility's resident brain surgeon, for an expert (and discreet) consultation. Shepherd agreed to keep the tests (and eventual surgery) under close wraps as much for the sake of confidentiality as the possibility for future professional opportunities, while Webber insisted that he didn't want to become part of the hospital's remarkably active rumor mill. (Strangely, this discretion did not carry over to season two, when Webber found himself publicly recovering at the hospital, even enlisting O'Malley to chronicle the staff's goings-on while he convalesced.)

Personal relationships, and especially romantic ones, are of paramount importance in episodic television; whom a character is attracted to and how he relates to him or her speaks volumes about the essential nature of who he is and why he does what he does. The ultimate irony of Dr. Webber was how he ended up actually being little or nothing like the man he purported to be, evidenced by the people with whom he dealt and the way he dealt with them. For example, rather than being a man of absolute certitude or moral correctness, Webber had an affair with Ellis Grey some seventeen years ago, but ultimately stayed in his marriage to Adele. The push-pull conflict between self-gratification and knowing (and doing) what's right always seems to be battling within him, whether he's insisting to be prematurely reinstated as a surgeon or conceding to the nurses' demands after their strike.

Webber is often confronted with the fact that hasty decisions can be wrong, and ends up changing his opinion or perception to allow for a more sensible conclusion. This has at times seemed due to the participation or, as he might perceive it, interference of his female colleagues and companions; seldom has he made a move without being corrected or second-guessed by someone on staff. Presumably this is derived at least in part by the show's concentration on female characters and their importance, but Webber's hen-pecked existence demonstrates an important cultural shift away from the (historically) indefatigable authority of male figures and toward a more balanced perception of the masculine and feminine impulses.

That, however, is not to say that he does not enjoy some of the same epiphanies that his young charges do. Though he originally enlisted Burke as temporary Chief because he thought the surgeon was "just like him," free from attachments and ready to assume the challenging and often lonely position at the top of the hospital food chain, Webber did not realize that his own observations were not only inaccurate but plain wrong. Not to mention his sanctimonious attitude toward Shepherd's affair with Meredith, which he judged seemingly without any regard for his own indiscretions. In this sense, he is a classic male—the man who faces his failures, overcomes them or discards them, and pushes forward to the next challenge. But no matter how readily Webber pretends that he is infallible, a man who answers to no one, there will always be a woman there—Dr. Bailey, his wife Adele, or even his intern Meredith—to remind him that's not the case.

GEORGE O'MALLEY

At the beginning of *Grey's Anatomy*, George was a little bit like a puppy dog—a creature who just wanted to love and be loved and keep the peace at any cost. It came as little surprise that the other characters quickly relegated him to the position of best friend, confidant, support system, or even just "the weaker kid," as Cristina pointedly called him. So why, then, has he become such an incredible source of fascination? In short, because watching him is like watching a boy become a man—or in other words, for women, seeing the guy who had a crush on you in junior high grow up to be the captain of the high school football team.

That isn't to say that his evolution hasn't been a bumpy one. Despite his insistence otherwise, George spent a lot of time being the sensitive pal to his female colleagues, or at least the guy they knew was totally "safe" if they needed to vent, be fragile, or otherwise let out their feelings. But some of George's most famous female encounters speak a lot more strongly to his masculinity than his more obvious feminine qualities; even his showdown with Meredith in "What Have I Done to Deserve This?" (2-19), which ended with her in tears and him leaving her house, demonstrated that George has a lot more old-fashioned guyness in him than the sort of sensitivity we might otherwise assume.

The two-part episode "It's the End of the World" and "(As We Know It)" (2-16 and 2-17) was a watershed moment in George's development, as it was for almost all the *Grey's* characters. As described in detail by creator Rhimes in the DVD commentaries, this was an episode where all the adults, or authority figures, were out of commission, leaving the interns, or "kids," much of the emotional heavy lifting. Since the beginning of the series, George was always the most childlike of the interns, even when he surpassed the limitations of childhood to demonstrate adult-level maturity and capability, as he did when he performed emergency heart surgery during the season two episode "Bring the Pain" (2-5). But during "(As We

45

Know It)," George was forced to face up to his adulthood and his owner-ship of the authority bestowed upon him by his job.

In the episode, Bailey arrived at the hotel ready to give birth, but refused to do so—endangering her baby—until her husband arrived. When she discovered that he was injured while driving to the hospital, she continued to resist, but George cannily convinced her that she was behaving contrary to the way "Dr. Bailey"—the unstoppable persona she had created as his mentor—normally would. He not only convinced her to proceed with labor, but helped her through the process, at the cost of some of the feeling in his right hand. It was in this moment that his adult masculinity—or at least the promise he showed to become a confident, decisive leader—finally emerges from his neuroses.

Later came George's disastrous encounter with Meredith, which failed for multiple reasons, not the least of which was that George was in many ways very much like her father. But his reaction—to run away and avoid all contact with Meredith—though outwardly immature or "feminine," was very much in keeping with masculine pride. Though he seldom succumbs to it, George is proud enough occasionally to be embarrassed, and his failed effort to win Meredith's heart showed a simultaneous disregard for the most plausible outcome (in his hope to gain reciprocity from someone who saw him exclusively as a friend) and the horrible realization that his desired outcome could not possibly be reached, even temporarily. Though not in so many words, George even admitted to this later in the series, indicating that he hoped blindly for an outcome that his common sense warned him wasn't possible. With his pride and self-perceived manhood compromised, he could not address or redress the incident with Meredith until his feelings of embarrassment subsided.

Ultimately, however, George has made some surprising strides toward the sort of rigid masculinity that defines his predecessors, while venturing away from the overwrought sensitivity that originally relegated his character to the role of show mascot. Like the rest of his male counterparts, George is a far more interesting and complicated guy than he was when we first saw him; at the very least, it's now a lot safer to actually call him a guy.

ALEX KAREV

Alex is in a lot of ways George's exact opposite: the character who initially embodied everything competitive, ambitious, and unfeeling about men. This, we discovered, was no more the case than George's personification of male "femininity." But Alex is an interesting case in that he very closely resembles that classic male model, and yet carries enough contradictions to catapult him into a place of genuine modernity—and further, male sensitivity.

During season one, Alex cultivated a reputation for being an aggressive, back-stabbing tough guy—so much so, in fact, that his nickname among his colleagues became "Dr. Evil Spawn," a designation that delighted him to no end. But his relationship with Izzie—seemingly purely physical at first—quickly demonstrated that Evil has more than one side. He tried to date her in earnest, wooing her with aggressive confidence and the certitude that he could provide for her whatever she needed or wanted. But just as real feelings began to develop between them, he suffered from several noteworthy setbacks: He learned that he failed his medical boards, which meant he might be kicked out of the surgical program, and he was subsequently unable to perform sexually due to the combination of that blow to his professional competence and the unexpected blossoming of genuine affection for Izzie.

He unfortunately combated this with some emotionally meaningless sex with a nurse, which Izzie walked in on. But it spoke directly to his masculine sense of compensation, and the sense that one can simply "correct" feelings of inadequacy, that he philandered in order to restore his mojo. Ironically, this tactic seemed to be effective: Unable to redeem himself with Izzie, he channeled his personal frustrations into an attack on George, then took them out on his other co-workers and even patients. His insistence on telling "the truth," essentially an excuse for the young doctor to be as cruel and insensitive as possible, temporarily relieved him from the pressure of embracing or otherwise dealing with his own feelings, and allowed him to function superficially on a professional level even as his real impulses bubbled beneath the surface.

Ultimately, Alex did show his true colors—in particular, his real sensitivity to others—when consoling Izzie after the death of a patient with whom she had become involved, even though they had been fighting for the past few weeks. His support and gentleness in these scenes suggested reservoirs of feeling that few if any audience members suspected that Alex actually had. But whether he continues to sustain this increased sensitivity remains to be seen as of this writing; for now, he remains a female fan favorite if for no other reason than the possibility that this tough guy will reveal his tender side.

DR. PRESTON BURKE

Preston Burke is one of the most interesting and complex male characters on *Grey's Anatomy*. He truly exemplifies the tenuous boundary between the classic male image and the reformed, sensitive male of metrosexual infamy: Though free and open with his feelings, Burke has a tendency to address issues or problems from an almost icily logical point of view, as if emotions should be "dealt" with in the same way ailing organs are in the operating room. Unfortunately, he seems to discover (and rediscover) that his own heart is frequently more fragile than can be easily repaired.

48

During season one, Burke's demeanor changed significantly; such is usually the case with TV shows, particularly when they begin to take on a life of their own and the characters become more or less appealing once the actors (not to mention other writers) offer their own interpretations. In the first episodes, Burke was cold, competitive, and not much else. In fact, Dr. Webber told him that his uncompromising demeanor was part of the reason that he was not the only candidate for replacing him as Chief of Surgery. Few could have expected how much Burke would take this conversation to heart. While its impact mainly manifested itself in his burgeoning relationship with Cristina Yang, the worry that he did not feel enough persisted in his struggle with his patients and co-workers on a recurrent basis.

For example, Burke's initial reaction to Shepherd was one of hostility and competitiveness—so much so, in fact, that he refused to call Shepherd (or allow Shepherd to call him) by his first name. But the cracks in his relentlessly professional façade appeared early: When he admitted an old friend and later discovered that the friend's wife was unfaithful, the love and displaced rejection for his friend was palpable.

But his generosity grew over the course of the series, culminating not only in his acceptance of friendship with Shepherd but in a great understanding of what his friends, colleagues, and loved ones need, best evidenced in the season two episodes "It's the End of the World" and "(As We Know It)" (2-16 and 2-17). In the two-parter, Burke selflessly awaited the removal of an explosive device buried in the chest of a patient; this, contrary to the outward designs of the episode, was not so he could save the day or be a hero. Rather, it was because he knew a terrified young woman—two of them, actually—had put herself in harm's way to save a patient, and he respected and wanted to reciprocate those efforts. Not only did Burke stay and talk to Meredith as she grew increasingly incoherent with fear, assuaging her distress with the patience and dedication of a professional surgeon, but he gave full credit for his eventual save of the man to Hannah Davies, a paramedic whose own crisis of confidence led her to risk everyone's death by removing her hand from the patient's chest before the bomb was removed.

49

Ultimately, however, it has been Burke's romance with Yang that has provided the show with its true emotional center, surpassing the showier romances of Izzie and Alex, and Derek and Meredith. Yang is nothing if not ambitious—she eats, sleeps, and breathes medicine—but she could stand to learn a lot from Burke, who one suspects is still learning all the things that he could be teaching her. During season one, for example, Burke slowly and quietly seduced Cristina, employing the sort of practicality that most women would find abhorrent but which proved amazingly effective on his chosen paramour. Their affair, consummated almost exclusively during downtime at the hospital, not only provided an interstitial text for the main thrust (no pun intended) of Meredith's McDreamy dilemma, but eventually offered a study in contrasts: Burke, much more certain about his place in life and work, was precise and accurate and determined to get the things he wants—all of them—and did not mince words when articulating his feelings or what he wants to do with them. And while Cristina struggled with what a romantic relationship could mean to her professional life (and does to her personal one), it was sometimes ironic given her own pragmatic sensibilities that she faltered beneath Burke's clinical approach to moving the relationship forward.

What continues to prove interesting between Burke and Cristina as the series progresses is just how the gender roles both switch constantly and are redefined, even within a modernized context. Burke, fearing that personal attachments would be an obstacle, broke up with Cristina, who was doubly confused because she was pregnant and had unresolved feelings about him. His coldness seemed to persist, however, when he recanted his earlier statement, not only seeking a reunion but a deeper relationship and eventually cohabitation. Funniest, however, was his own seeming inability to reconcile his sense of logic with his sense of love; erupting at her for refusing to give up her own apartment and move in with him, he delivered a list of professional credentials, insisting that he was in complete control of his life, and yet could not maintain even a tenuous feeling of certainty when it came to his relationship with Cristina.

But as this relationship matured in the eyes of the audience, we continued to see important glimmers of the sensitive man lurking beneath his sometimes machinelike exterior: laughing to keep from crying when telling a patient that he fixed his "broken heart"; buddying up with George after his disastrous romantic interlude with Meredith; poignantly withdrawing after failing to save the musician who inspired him to become a doctor. Burke is perhaps the most real and fully realized of the show's male characters. Even if, God forbid, an explosive device did actually go off, ridding the show of its female leads and the outward reason to retain viewers, *Grey's Anatomy* would still be worth watching— even if Burke were stuck lying incapacitated in a hospital bed.

THE MODERN MAN REDEFINED

With so much complexity, who else just wants to pick one or the other— the classic leading man or the sensitive modern male—and be done with it? Certainly it would be easier for men (and women) in real life. But until the day that romantic relationships become uncomplicated, or people can separate their physical needs from their emotional ones, a clear winner is not likely to emerge from this equally complicated age-old conflict.

Should audiences pick the tough guy whose feelings just need to be coaxed out of hiding? Or the sensitive schlub who secretly wants some adversity to toughen him up? This problem has haunted viewers since way before Big, and will lurk in the corners of their hearts long after the last episode of *Grey's Anatomy* has aired. Perhaps Bailey answered the dilemma best: "It's not hard. It's painful, but it's not hard. You know what to do already; if you didn't you wouldn't be in so much pain" ("Bring the Pain," 2-5). If we can figure out what that means, then maybe we have a chance of choosing the right one.

TODD GILCHRIST is a Los Angeles-based writer who has worked for more than ten years as a film, music, and TV critic. Currently employed by IGN.com as the Movies Senior Editor, he has previously contributed to numerous Web sites and print publications, including *The Miami New Times*, Filmstew.com, *Starburst Magazine*, and Scifi.com among others. Todd's reviews have also appeared in collegiate-level textbooks such as *Reading Culture: Contexts for Critical Reading and Writing*, and he is a member of the Los Angeles Film Critics Association.

Forget the used-so-often-the-very-idea-is-cliché doctor show premise—
Grey's is a new kind of television series. Part mainstream hit, part cult
phenomenon, it has the rating numbers that networks drool over and
the kind of fan love that gratifies everyone involved. It's the sort of success every network exec wishes he or she could duplicate. Don't worry,
guys—Sarah Wendell's taking notes.

Sarah Wendell

DIAGNOSTIC NOTES, CASE HISTORIES, AND PROFILES OF ACUTE HYBRIDITY IN *GREY'S ANATOMY*

*Subject presents with symptoms in discord: high ratings and
position as top ten primetime show contrast with cult devotion
and frequent online involvement by fans in show plotlines.
"Coolness" factor rising through innovative episode topics, but
popularity increase may cause decrease in same factor, and
decrease total numbers of dedicated fanbase viewership of show.
Possible diagnosis: hybrid blend of cult show with mainstream
success, yielding unique position in television. Will continue to
observe for further consult. Case history attached.*

CASE HISTORY: THE PRECARIOUS HEALTH OF CULT TELEVISION SHOWS

In the days before DVD releases, digital video recorders, and the Internet,
it was relatively easy to tell the difference between a mainstream hit TV
show and a cult TV show. The mainstream show was the television program that a majority of viewers in a timeslot or an age group watched on
a somewhat regular basis. It was, to borrow a phrase from NBC, "Must-
See TV." The cult show was the offbeat, underground show that only a
handful of people watched, but that handful was vocal, involved with one

another, and could potentially be found dressing up as the show's characters. The cult show was often a short-lived series that rarely reappeared on television, while the mainstream show could go on for seasons before then moving into perpetual syndication. To twist a joke about cult films, "a mainstream show is seen one time by 1,000 people; a cult show is seen 1,000 times by one person" ("Cult Classic").

Diagnostically speaking, with the current television lineup it's much more difficult to say what's a cult hit, what's a mainstream hit, and what's in between. Viewers of CSI often discuss in-depth on online message boards the science techniques used in recent episodes, a devotion that would seem "cultish" on the surface, and yet CSI and all its variations are top-ten shows in the current ratings. Shoppers hunting DVD shelves for new releases of television shows will find the most recent seasons of currently popular shows alongside old shows resurrected from seasons long past. Cult shows and mainstream shows have started to occupy the same territory, not just in stores but in ratings as well, and many currently on the air occupy a divergent category: part cult, part mainstream.

54   *Grey's Anatomy* is an example of how a show can be exceptionally popular and yet maintain a fanbase that is dedicated to such a point that even the media comments on its "cult following" (Deimen). Shows like *Grey's Anatomy* have hybridized the concept of a cult show with that of a mainstream popular show and created an entirely new category, which requires in turn a new diagnosis and definition that adequately represents the fanbase dedicated to the show while also acknowledging the population numbers of that fanbase, which propel the show into high ratings week after week.

Identifying and classifying what makes a show "mainstream" is an obvious prospect. It begins with ratings, continues with ratings, and ends with position on the week's top-ten list of watched shows: again, ratings. *Grey's Anatomy*, already popular since its debut as a mid-season replacement, shot into the top five most-watched shows and gained an enormous boost after winning the post-Super-Bowl timeslot on February 5, 2006 (Ryan, Aug. 17). Prior to the Super Bowl show, which marks a decided turning point in the ratings, *Grey's Anatomy* averaged between 16 and 17 million viewers (Ryan, Sep. 11). After the Super Bowl show, which featured a much-advertised and mysterious nude shower scene,

Grey's Anatomy experienced a 36 percent jump in ratings, from 17.9 million viewers, itself not a shabby number, to 22.5 million viewers (Ryan, Aug. 17). *Grey's Anatomy* suddenly occupied ratings territory previously inhabited only by *Desperate Housewives* and *American Idol*, the current powerhouse shows of primetime.

The mathematical evidence of *Grey's Anatomy*'s status as a mainstream hit is simple to quantify, and present methods of measurement confirm the diagnosis of immense popularity. However, existing definitions used to diagnose a cult show do not adequately measure subjects like *Grey's Anatomy*. A most insightful, though unedited and repetitive, definition for "cult television show" can be found on Wikipedia, itself an audience-driven cult phenomenon. Wikipedia's writers identify a "cult television show" as a show that has a "strong loyal audience that thinks a lot about the show," and "encourages its viewers to do more than just sit and watch it" ("Cult Television"). Moreover, the show should "achieve a moderate level of popularity," though the entry further cautions that "obscurity often makes shows more popular with intense fans" ("Cult Television"). The fans of cult television shows can also use their personal involvement to seek out other like-minded fans through conventions and informal gatherings or, since the arrival of the Internet, chat rooms, bulletin boards, and fan Web sites. Further evidence of a cult following can be found in the prevalence of "fanfic," or fan fiction, wherein devotees of a show pen their own scripts and scenarios for characters outside of the story arcs of the show itself, often pairing characters romantically or heightening sexual tension between existing pairs.

A preliminary search of Internet-based fan communities devoted to *Grey's Anatomy* yields a variety of options for an individual seeking discussion or interaction with other devotees of the show. From fan forums hosted at existing community-building sites such as Xanga and Blogger, to independent sites located at *Grey's Anatomy*-related URLs based on variations of the show title, such as greys-media.com and greysanatomyinsider.com, the options available indicate a high number of fans seeking a virtual gathering place to foster involvement beyond solitary viewing of the show. As for the presence of fanfic depositories online, *Grey's Anatomy* also meets this criterion, with fan-written scripts and short stories appearing at the fanfic clearinghouse Fanfic.net in topic-based communities such as "BANG," which

55

features Preston Burke/Cristina Yang stories, and "Derridith," devoted to pieces addressing the romance between Derek Shepherd and Meredith Grey.

A similar and rather tongue-in-cheek diagnosis of "cult status" can be found at Everything2.com. The article's content primarily addresses the more obscure and devoted fans of cult shows who dress up as their favorite character, attend conferences devoted to the world in which the show is set, and perhaps live a portion of their lives within the alternate reality of the show itself. While these indications of cult status do not apply to *Grey's Anatomy*, the initial description of the term does. The author, "drdave," defines the concept of "cult status" very succinctly:

> Cult status is, in effect, a simple acknowledgement of social/intellectual achievement obtained by an individual, his work, or both. The major difference between cult status and any other acknowledgement of public recognition (such as plain stardom) is that it focuses on quality rather than quantity within the support base.

56

Before going on to poke a bit of fun at those who spend many waking hours on their devotion to a show, "drdave" does point out something that the Wikipedia definition lacks: The attention paid a cult show is not due to the show's popularity or lack thereof, but rather the quality of the show itself. The acknowledgment of quality that "drdave" mentions is of paramount importance in creating a new definition of "cult" entertainment, because *Grey's Anatomy's* position as a popular show and as a cult show hinges on the creative individuals developing that quality: the writers.

A new definition of the modern cult television show has to be assembled to classify this show accurately largely because of the blog, Grey Matter, created by the writing team behind *Grey's Anatomy*. The blog illustrates the primary difference between old cult shows and the current style of cult entertainment: the writers' intimate, daily involvement with the audience both inspires fans to get involved beyond merely watching, and invites more people in greater numbers to tune in and watch the show. Certainly ratings are one option of measurement of the quality of a show, but, as any fan of a long-dead cult show will attest, quality doesn't necessarily guarantee ratings or guard against cancellation. What makes shows like *Grey's Anatomy* unique as a cult phenomenon is the attention paid by the fans to the individual writers themselves. Often the actors of a show serve as emissaries for their program; with *Grey's Anatomy*, the writers also have cult followings of their own, and they themselves act as representatives of their work.

Television writers enjoying a devoted fanbase is a relatively new symptom of growing tendencies toward cult status in the world of television production, and began most notably with *Buffy the Vampire Slayer*, itself a well-known cult show with a large and devoted following. In an interview with the Web magazine PopGurls, television writer David Fury traces the history of fan admiration of writers, beginning with his own experience as a writer and co-executive producer for *Buffy the Vampire Slayer*:

> There's never been a show, to my knowledge, in which the writers developed their own followings. Audiences generally don't recognize script-driven shows, and when they do, they tend to credit the show's creator(s) and showrunner for every episode, regardless of whose name was on the script (Amy).

Fury discusses in the interview the value of a writer interacting with the audience online in fan forums and communities, since both *Buffy* and its spin-off *Angel* had producer- and writer-initiated fan forums of their own. Fury himself was "responsible for the creation of 'The Fuselage,' the *Lost* fansite," and says that the immediate feedback of viewers can be very satisfying for television writers. Further, Fury attests that the interaction with the viewers can encourage the writers' "work environment to be a happy, supportive place. That's why *Grey's Anatomy* is "enjoying the interaction" between what he calls the "creative team" and the fans. The writers know immediately that the show they're creating is enjoyed by the audience, and reap the benefits of immediate gratification before the ratings are posted. Thus, *Grey's Anatomy* follows in the Internet footsteps of *Buffy the Vampire Slayer* and its prominent cult spin-off *Angel*, which both had active online communities where show writers interacted frequently with viewers.

On the Grey Matter writers' blog, the writers deliberately cultivate a relationship with their viewers, encouraging them to respond and discuss the storylines, episodes, and characters. The writers even discuss reruns as they reappear, a task that came as a spur-of-the moment decision from series creator, writer, and executive producer Shonda Rhimes. In the Frequently Asked Questions section, or "FAQ," appearing on ABC's page devoted to *Grey's Anatomy*, when asked if the writers' blog would continue over the summer hiatus, Rhimes wrote:

> I do love to blog with you all. I really do. But I'm gonna be spending the summer writing episodes and so, until we air again, you probably won't be hearing from me. Wait. Just now, I had an idea. We (the writers) can blog the first season reruns of *Grey's Anatomy* the same way we blogged the second season (Rhimes).

Thus, over the summer of 2006, as season one of *Grey's Anatomy* was replayed on ABC, the writers took turns discussing the behind-the-scenes development of each episode as they each looked back on the first season. The writers wrote entries about each second season episode as it debuted, but revisiting the first season in reruns a year after it aired revealed a great deal about the writing community behind the show and invited the audience to participate on a much more intimate level. Their efforts also kept the blog content current and updated, which is absolutely crucial to maintaining repeat visitors who look for new content, but which also invited the readers and viewers to appreciate the writers as human individuals working to create a television show. Writer Krista Vernoff revisited the first episode she wrote for *Grey's Anatomy* when it aired for the second time on July 27, 2006, and began her entry by telling the readers where, and who, she was when the show first started in season one:

> Shonda just told me we're blogging season one as they repeat this summer. BLOGGING SEASON ONE. Seriously, do you know how long ago season one was. . . ? Okay, here's what I remember: I remember that we all met, this bedraggled group

of writers, for the most part all coming from other recently cancelled shows. I myself had come from a sweet little show called *Wonderfalls* that Fox killed after airing only three episodes.

Vernoff goes on to describe her process when writing the episode "If Tomorrow Never Comes" (1-6) and defending the decision to kill off an ancillary character in that episode as part of a larger theme about seizing the moment: "Believe it or not, we actually do think about what kind of message we put into the world" (Vernoff). By inviting the viewers to examine her decision and by explaining the reasons why she wrote that plot twist, Vernoff, and the other writers who described episodes they wrote for season one, create an intimacy that doesn't normally exist between writers and viewers. Because of the writers' blog, the viewers know not only what happened on the episode they just watched, but *why* it happened as well.

Further taking advantage of new technology, the show's writers also host podcasts, which are individual audio programs available for download and recorded specifically for playback on mp3 players. Rhimes's FAQ answers viewers' requests for more information about the show by inviting them to listen to the podcasts as an additional resource to the blog, stating that the podcasts feature "different interviews each week with actors, writers, exec producers, editors, etc. They . . . give you a lot of insight into how much fun the actors really are or exactly what the heck the writers are thinking" (Rhimes). Divulging so much behind-the-scenes information and engaging the viewers in the process behind the finished product reveals a cult community on the other side of the show as well: The writers are equally as committed to their interaction with the audience as the audience is to the show's backstage revelations.

Ironically, the most useful element in maintaining *Grey's Anatomy*'s cult audience, despite the amply provided behind-the-scenes details, is the secrecy surrounding the writing of the show. While on one hand there is an extraordinary variety of detail about the process of creating the show, series creator Shonda Rhimes is equally devoted to maintaining secrecy about future plot twists and storylines. In the ABC FAQ,

Rhimes is asked if it's possible to visit the writers' room while the team is in action, and her answer is an unequivocal no:

> Our writers' room is super-secret, incredibly crazy, sacred place [sic]. It is Narnia. It is Oz. It is . . . well, some other place it's really difficult to get into. In that room . . . we come up with the storylines for the season. . . . No one gets in. Not the press, not the actors, and—I'm sorry—not you. You might have heard that I am obsessive about secrecy. It's true. I am.

The deliberate guarding of detail is the attraction that keeps the Internet-lurking fanbase coming back for more information. *Grey's Anatomy* is not a show with a large mystery at its core, such as *Lost* or *24*. There are backstories that have yet to be disclosed, but there is no central mystery to the series. The secrecy masked in divulged information fosters continued involvement from viewers, who return to the blog and other fan sites to try to guess and glean from the bits of revealed detail what will happen on the show. Tempting viewers with multiple puzzles in the form of character backstory and future story allows for a continued unchecked growth in fans' cult involvement.

Because plotlines and upcoming stories are kept so secret, the hints and insights delivered through the creative team's online blog communication with the viewers also serve to heighten the sense of connection to the individual staff members who write the episodes. Much like the devotees of *Buffy the Vampire Slayer*, the *Grey's Anatomy* fans know the first names of the individuals who comprise the team. Rhimes herself reveals the names and contributions of writers and even assistants in the FAQ, and gives credit on that page and in the blog for their efforts by divulging how certain terms that have become part of *Grey's Anatomy*'s vernacular ended up in the scripts, such as "va-jay-jay," or the use of the word "seriously" as punctuation to a sentence (Rhimes). Beyond the issue of recognition, however, fans on a first-name basis with the writers of a show also have someone to hold accountable when storylines take a direction of which they don't approve, and get a sense of how the writers work in the viewers' interest by lobbying the network to allow them to air a controversial storyline.

The writers' blog, and the fans' knowledge that the writers, particularly Rhimes herself, read all the comments left at that site, solidifies the sense of camaraderie, showing fans that the team creating the show is as interested in viewers' opinions as they are in crafting the show. The blog cultivated the cult audience, while the secrecy maintained in the midst of all that divulgence further maintained that audience's interest, even as the number of people watching continued to increase by the millions. The writers' enthusiasm for their show, coupled with the audience's similar enthusiasm, yields a unique phenomenon: a dual-sided cult fanbase. The creation of that virtual friendship between the fans and the writers is the signature element to creating a cult audience out of a very popular show.

TREATMENT AND PROGNOSIS: CONTEMPORARY CULT TELEVISION SHOWS

Blogs and online communities developed by the creative team behind *Grey's Anatomy* are the foundation to establishing the previously dichotomous state between cult and mainstream, and are the reason a new definition is needed to fully describe and diagnose this type of show. A show's blog can both reveal and conceal the future of the show, teasing viewers to increase their involvement in the show. Whereas cult fans can be fickle and might otherwise abandon a show after it gains notoriety and popularity, the behind-the-scenes revelations give viewers the opportunity to guess what will happen, to remain engaged, even as the overall viewer numbers continue to grow. And while a mainstream show can easily become subject to the pressure of success and demands from a network, a communication channel as simple as a blog can let the audience know that the writers, who care about the characters as much as the fans do, are still working on crafting a story they admire. Based on the tone of the *Grey's Anatomy* writers' blog, the writers are as much cult fans of the show as the viewers are, with both groups having an interest in furthering involvement beyond just writing or just watching. It's not *just a job* for the writers, it seems, and it's not *just entertainment* for the viewers.

Diagnosing *Grey's Anatomy* as both a cult and a mainstream show despite or because of its popularity onscreen and online also creates a protocol for identifying other opportunities to cultivate a cult audience for already-popular programs—to create, to coin a term, a "cult/pop" show. Shows like *Grey's Anatomy* should serve as models for diagnosis of cult/pop status. If a potential cult audience, no matter its size, is provided with the ability to connect with one another and, better still, with the individuals behind the show, that audience will respond with continued involvement. Unlike cult shows of the older model, whose audiences may have abandoned a show when it gained mainstream popularity, a cultivated cult audience of a popular show can continue to remain attentive so long as the folks on the backstage side of production continue their involvement.

In the case of *Grey's Anatomy*, the genuine regard demonstrated by the writers for their creation matches the devotion of the viewers. So long as the communication between the two groups remains active, *Grey's Anatomy* will not go the way of shows whose audiences became disenchanted or fade away due to the burden of its own popularity, since, as a cult/pop show, it blends the power of high ratings with a continually fascinated and active audience.

SARAH WENDELL is a transplanted Pittsburgher currently living in the New York metropolitan area. By day she's mild-mannered and heavily caffeinated. By evening she dons her cranky costume, consumes yet more caffeine, and becomes Smart Bitch Sarah of Smart Bitches, Trashy Books. The site specializes in reviewing romance novels, examining the history and future of the genre, and bemoaning the enormous prevalence of bodacious pectorals adorning male cover models.

Sarah has B.A.s in English and Spanish from Columbia College of South Carolina. She is a member of the Romance Writers of America, and a big, big fan of Fabio.

REFERENCES

Amy. "PopGurls Interview: David Fury." *PopGurls*. 11 Sep. 2006.
    <http://www.popgurls.com/article_show.php3?id=591>

Collier, Aldore. "Shonda Rhimes: The Force Behind *Grey's
    Anatomy.*"*Ebony*. 13 Sep. 2006. <http://www.findarticles.com/p/
    articles/mi_m1077/is_12_60/ai_n15632370>.

"Cult Classic" *Wikipedia, The Free Encyclopedia*. 12 Jan. 2007.
    <http://en.wikipedia.org/wiki/Cult_classic>

"Cult Following." *Wikipedia, The Free Encyclopedia*. 11 Sep. 2006.
    <http://en.wikipedia.org/wiki/Cult_following>

"Cult Television." *Wikipedia, The Free Encyclopedia*. 31 Aug. 2006.
    <http://en.wikipedia.org/wiki/Cult_television>

Deimen, Justin. "Grey's Anatomy." *The Urban Wire*. 12 Sep. 2006.
    <http://www.theurbanwire.com/stories/index.php?option=com_content&tas
    k=view&id=549&Itemid=67>

Drdave. "Cult Status." *Everything2.com*. 12 Sep. 2006. <http://www.every-
    thing2.com/index.pl?node_id=1482149&displaytype=printable>

M_ruv. "Stick a Fork in It." *TVgasm*. 14 Sep. 2006.
    <http://www.tvgasm.com/archives/greys_anatomy/001788.php>

Rhimes, Shonda. "Frequently Asked Questions Answered by Shonda Rhimes."
    ABC.com. 13 Sep. 2006. <http://abc.go.com/primetime/greysanatomy/faq.html>

Ryan, Joal. "'Anatomy' of Super Sunday." *E!Online*. 11 Sep. 2006.
    <http://www.eonline.com/News/Items/0,17696,00.html>

Ryan, Joal. "*Grey's Anatomy* Still on Super High." *E!Online*. 17 Aug. 2006.
    <http://www.eonline.com/News/Items/0,1,18567,00.html>

Vernoff, Krista. "Krista Vernoff on Writing Her First Episode." *Grey Matter*. 29
    Oct. 2006. <http://www.greyswriters.com/2006/07/krista_vernoff_.html>

63

If real sex is like the sex you see on most network television, then everyone I know is a virgin. Not so with the sex on *Grey's*. Here, Jacqueline Carey celebrates the show's realistic depiction of sex in all its quirky permutations: sex you fall asleep during, sex you have while drunk, sex you have in supply closets during bomb scares. . . .

Jacqueline Carey

SEX IN SEATTLE

Remember Dr. Ruth?

Back in the 1980s, this tiny woman with a thick German accent broke new ground, first in radio and then in television programming, giving candid sex advice. My *most* vivid memory . . . well, my most vivid memory is hearing her read a viewer's letter and exclaim, "Tree people? What's all this about sex with tree people?" After my wild mental image of human limbs and leafy branches intertwining in carnal-sylvan bliss, trunks and torsos heaving, hair and foliage tossing, finally subsided, I realized Dr. Ruth was responding to a question about a *ménage à trois*. For younger readers, that's what we used to call threesomes (or *tree*somes, if you have a thick German accent) back in the day when it wasn't practically a rite of passage. Now you can flip on MTV's "The Real World" and watch random trios of drunken young people fall into bed together without a second thought, groping and giggling. But in days of yore, when hair was big and frizzy, and acid-washed jeans and legwarmers seemed like a good idea, the threesome still held an air of mystery and was spoken of in hushed French whispers.

Anyway, I digress.

My second most vivid memory is of reading a review of Dr. Ruth's television show, which marveled over one simple fact: This little old lady (okay, she was just pushing sixty, but that was old to me at the time) with the funny accent was doing something radical. She was talking about sex as though it were a perfectly normal act performed with considerable frequency by consenting adults. Well, hallelujah!

I think Dr. Ruth Westheimer would approve of *Grey's Anatomy*. Sure, it's hardly the first TV show of its kind. *Grey's* hails from a long and venerable line of medical soap operas, but I would argue that it's unique—and refreshingly frank—in its approach to human sexuality, and in particular to female sexuality. Sure, *Sex and the City* went there first, but it aired on HBO. This is primetime network television.

The women of Seattle Grace get laid. A lot. Without apologies.

And sometimes it's great, sometimes it's good, sometimes it's mediocre, and sometimes it's downright horrible. In two seasons, *Grey's Anatomy* has covered a wider spectrum of the human sexual experience than most regular network shows cover over their entire run.

I'm not talking about the Kinsey Scale; *Grey's* main characters thus far seem firmly rooted in heterosexual territory. And I'm not talking about the spectrum ranging from plain vanilla, missionary-style sex to whatever Chunky Monkey mango nutmeg rum raisin moniker you want to hang on full-bore, "Honey, climb into the sling and I'll get the ball-gag and the feather tickler" sex. No, what *Grey's* has done so well is explore the human experience of sex; the physical, psychological, and emotional ramifications of it. How it affects marriages, friendships, and love affairs. Why we do it. Why we don't do it. Why sometimes we do it and wish we hadn't.

The ill-advised hook-up between Meredith and George in the second season is an outstanding example of the latter. He was besotted with her; she was an emotional wreck, still dealing with the fall-out of being dumped by McDreamy and the more recent trauma of seeing her absent father for the first time in twenty years. George offered up his adoration as balm, Meredith reached for him for comfort . . . which in Meredith's world means sex. The episode faded to black as millions of viewers groaned.

Why? Because it wasn't Hairy Back Guy or Tattooed Guy or Inappropriate Facial Hair Guy, or any one of the disposable, nameless one-night-stands with whom Meredith has consoled herself. It was

George, with his puppy-dog eyes and his desperate crush on Meredith. He adored her; she was fond of him. There were feelings involved. And you knew, you just knew, it was going to end badly.

And oh, did it ever! The following episode made it clear that what happened was a mistake, but it did a great job of drawing out the suspense until revealing the dire deed itself in a flashback. It was awful. It was beyond awful. Mid-coitus, Meredith burst into tears and asked George, "You're almost done, right?"

And millions of viewers cringed.

These things happen in the real world. As *Grey's* creator Shonda Rhimes says in the official *Grey's Anatomy* FAQ, "In movies and most TV shows, when two friends sleep together, it's a magical start to a wonderful relationship. In life, it's quite often a hideous beginning to a very long awkward nightmare." People make terrible choices in intimacy and realize them at the most inopportune times. We hurt one another involuntarily with reactions we can't hide and feelings we can't deny.

But that's only one example. There's all kinds of sex on *Grey's*—it is, after all, a soap opera. There's casual sex, there's gotta-have-you sex, there's guilty sex, there's feed-the-beast sex, there's desperate-for-attention sex, there's end-of-the-world sex, there's even boring sex. The nature of the sex is in constant flux as relationships evolve and change.

That was evident from the get-go. The series announced its presence by introducing us to a heroine hurriedly attempting to banish her one-night stand so she could get to her internship on time. That's ballsy writing—but Shonda Rhimes wasn't afraid of creating characters who reflected reality. In an interview for the *Chicago Tribune*, Rhimes says, "Women can be flawed, nasty, strong, good. The definition of female is as broad as the definition of male."

Of course, as loyal viewers know, the one-night stand turned out to be The One: McDreamy himself, Derek Shepherd, head of neurosurgery at Seattle Grace. The relationship between Meredith and Derek is the lynch-pin of the series, and the sex between them progressed from tawdry to passionate to tender and romantic . . . and then back around to steamy and illicit in the finale of the second season.

Meanwhile, everyone around them was getting his or her freak on, with varying degrees of success. Cristina and Burke have a great physical

67

and intellectual connection, but they've got to get past the sex and surgery to figure out how to forge a genuine emotional partnership. Izzie and Alex perform a will-they, won't-they dance, interrupted by impotence, punctuated by extreme horniness (and the kind of ardent coupling that takes place when you might all get blown up by a bomb), derailed by Denny, the charming but doomed heart patient. And poor George is struggling to come to terms with the fact that while Meredith doesn't feel that way about him, he may well be someone else's McDreamy.

The Ghost of Sex Past haunts the show, too. Addison's infidelity and her attempts to save her marriage to Derek mirror Chief of Surgery Webber's affair with Meredith's mother and his subsequent return to his wife. No one is blameless, but *Grey's* manages to withhold passing judgment on its characters. It realizes that everyone makes mistakes, that sometimes we do the wrong things for the right reasons, and the right things for the wrong reasons. And sometimes we just plain screw up.

Everyone is flawed.

Everyone has sex.

And it has repercussions. It results in venereal diseases. It results in pregnancies, wanted and unwanted. It blows unacknowledged obstacles out of its urgent path, and it forges awkward silences between relative strangers who've gotten too intimate too fast. It can be a flash-point for an all-consuming romance or a terrible marker of the distance that has grown between two people. It brings people together and it tears them apart. It shows them things they'd rather not know about themselves and each other. It forces them to grow in ways that may be painful.

It's a part of the human condition. And sure, sometimes they take it to extremes; it is a soap opera. But watching *Grey's Anatomy*, you'd almost begin to think that sex was an act performed with considerable frequency between consenting adults, and that that's perfectly normal.

Hallelujah.

68

JACQUELINE CAREY is the bestselling author of the critically acclaimed Kushiel's Legacy trilogy of historical fantasy novels and the Sundering epic fantasy duology. Jacqueline enjoys doing research on a wide variety of arcane topics, and an affinity for travel has taken her from Finland to Egypt to date. She currently lives in west Michigan, where she is a member of the oldest Mardi Gras krewe in the state. Although often asked by inquiring fans, she does not, in fact, have any tattoos.

REFERENCES

Rhimes, Shonda. *"Grey's Anatomy* FAQ." *Grey's Anatomy.* Sep. 2006.
    <http://abc.go.com/primetime/greysanatomy/page?pn=faq>
Ryan, Maureen. "Chicago as 'Grey' Area?" *The Watcher.* 30 Sep. 2006.
    <http://featuresblogs.chicagotribune.com/entertainment_tv/2005/09/the_win
    dy_citys.htm>

The sex might be great, but at Seattle Grace love, as Eileen Rendahl points out, stinks. When our favorite interns fall in love, it inevitably ends badly: Unexpected wives show up, brand-new heart transplants have unforeseen repercussions, the ability to consummate one's relationship . . . well . . . you know. Picking up strange men in bars seems almost safe in comparison. Why bother to look for love at all?

Eileen Rendahl

LOVE STINKS

Meredith Grey had me at "I'm kinda screwed" ("A Hard Day's Night," 1-1).

When I heard those words, I felt a little bit as if I'd found a soul mate. I watched Meredith get up and cast around for her clothes and I felt for her. I don't know how many times I've woken up and felt that from the moment I opened my eyes that day, the odds were stacked against me. Like Meredith, who still struggled into that shirt and pants and tried to shoo that guy out the door, I still got up and faced whatever it was in front of me. So when she said she was kinda screwed, I got it. From that first breathy narration, I was rooting for Meredith. I felt totally connected to her. She was my kind of woman. She was strong and determined, a little bit vulnerable and . . .

. . . a little bit slutty. Yeah. That's what I said. Slutty. There was that guy, the dreamy one whose name she couldn't quite remember, from whom she'd clearly gotten what she needed and whom she now wanted *out out out* by the time she'd finished showering.

I can so relate.

I don't want to defend the excesses of the late seventies and early eighties, but the fact that sex couldn't actually kill you back then created a really different attitude toward it than is out there now. Being a little bit slutty back then wasn't so dangerous, and it had its moments when it could be an awful lot of fun, which is why I completely understand why Meredith Grey would, on her first night back in Seattle, getting ready to start her residency, go out and pick up a strange guy in a bar, sleep with him, and then kick him the hell out.

Meredith hadn't even unpacked her boxes yet (and wouldn't until Izzie and George moved in during a later episode), but she had made time to troll a bar and find a guy who was a cute enough catch to haul home. She could have had a lot of reasons for doing this. Maybe unpacking bored her and she decided to do a little mattress dancin' to pass the time. Maybe she was back in a house that didn't hold very good memories and increased her sense of being alone and she didn't want to feel lonely for that one night. Maybe she had an itch that needed scratching in a very particular way.

Yeah, maybe. Or maybe not. My guess as to why Meredith Grey went out that night and brought home a guy is this: to make herself feel powerful before she took on the next huge challenge of the extremely challenging career path that she had chosen. She knew how much strength walking that path would take. She watched her mother do it. She knew she would need to tap into every ounce of power she had.

There is nothing that makes a woman feel more powerful than knowing she can attract the opposite sex with nothing much more than a crook of her finger. This is especially true of a woman with daddy issues and, boy, does our buddy Meredith ever have daddy issues. It wasn't obvious in the first few moments of that first episode, but it didn't take long for us to learn that Meredith's father hadn't been part of her life for years and years. That alone pretty much guarantees some daddy issues for most people. To say that Meredith's go deeper and are more complicated than that is like saying that the Middle East has some hostility issues. At any rate, in my personal experience, for a woman with daddy issues, interest from the opposite sex is like catnip to kitties, like porno to fourteen-year-old boys, like the buttered side of my bread to the floor—you get the picture. It's a magnetic attraction that's hard to fight.

And why should Meredith fight it? We all know it feels good to make heads turn as we walk through a room. It makes us feel strong. It reminds us of our female might and that some of that might comes from being sexual creatures. Generally speaking, it's not always good to make your heroine slutty. It's not considered by most to be a particularly hero-ic quality. It's also a lot more common than most people truly want to admit. Even if you haven't made a lifetime career of it, who amongst us has never done something a little bit slutty? Or maybe even a lot bit slut-ty? Besides, it's not like Meredith is out there looking for Mr. Goodbar. Her sluttiness isn't wildly self-destructive. The guy she brings home on her wild fling? He's not a psychotic ax-wielding sadist. He's a neurosur-geon. If my mother had thought trolling for guys in bars was an effec-tive way to reel in a neurosurgeon boyfriend, she would probably have sent me out with a fake I.D. and fishnet hose when I was sixteen.

No, Meredith's flirtation with sluttiness isn't going to kill her. In fact, Meredith is just fine when she's slutty. The guys may not be just fine — remember the guy with the broken penis? — but sluttiness helps Meredith cope. It helps her stay focused on her goals without getting caught up in all that emotional love stuff that baffles her completely. Sluttiness helps her get over her hurt. Because Meredith gets hurt bad. Seriously bad. It happened when she stopped being slutty and fell in love, making herself vulnerable by openly giving her heart to Derek Shepherd. Who turned out to be married.

73

It was when she actually fell in love that our sweet Meredith crashed and burned. If she'd been able to sleep with McDreamy and then keep on walking as planned (remember at the beginning of that first episode when she told him she was going up to take a shower and that he should be gone by the time she was finished?), she would never have gotten her heart broken, jeopardized her career, or become an object of gossip for the rest of the hospital.

I'm not sure you could be punished worse for falling in love with someone than by finding out he's married to someone else because his spouse has just waltzed into your place of work and said, "And you must be the woman who's screwing my husband" ("Who's Zoomin' Who?," 1-9). That's the kind of shock and betrayal that can kill a person. Or sim-ply crush her to the point that she might wish she were dead.

As bad as that moment was, Meredith's punishment for having actu-ally fallen in love wasn't over. There was her devastating plea for Derek to choose her over Addison. Then there was Derek actually choosing

Addison over Meredith. There was everybody knowing everything about it, too. What did our buddy Meredith do to get over this string of hurts? She brought home a string of men. One after another, they spent the night, and then she sent them packing as if they were some kind of promiscuity penicillin that could cleanse her system of the love bug that had clearly infected her. I get her reasoning. Back in college, we always used to say the best way to get over one man was to get under another.

What can I say? It was the early eighties.

I realize that this is not a good feminist stance to take. Our power is supposed to come from our brains and our hearts, not our racks and our firm little asses (which I'm pretty sure I left behind in the early eighties, too). Meredith has a fantastic brain. They generally don't let dumb bunnies be surgeons. And heart? She's got plenty of that. In fact, maybe she has a little too much heart. Maybe all the residents at Seattle Grace do, and they all have trouble because of it.

Safety in sluttiness seems to be a pattern for the residents at Seattle Grace. Alex Karev, who loved Izzie enough to give her that long slow burning kiss in the middle of the Emerald City Bar in front of God and everybody and can apparently get it up for every nurse in the hospital, wilted like a hothouse rose in the Arizona sun when he was in bed with the object of his desire. What was up with that? Clearly, he was fine when it didn't matter. When it did matter and matter a lot, it was too much pressure for him. It wasn't just sex. It was love, and that's infinitely more dangerous, more dangerous even than sexually transmitted diseases, and those things can kill you.

And look at poor Izzie! When Alex cheated on her, she was angry, but she went on. She wasn't in love with him. She was just in lust. With whom did she fall in love? Denny Duquette, a man with a clinically broken heart. Izzie gave her love to a man with a heart so broken that he had to have an artificial one. As much as Denny wanted to give Izzie everything she was giving to him, he couldn't. Not really. All he could offer was a damaged organ shored up by a machine. So they played dirty Scrabble instead of having sex. When Denny was on the brink of death, Izzie was willing to throw away everything she had worked for to try and fix him. But she couldn't. He was beyond fixing. Letting him go squashed Izzie so completely that it broke her will to continue following her dream of being a surgeon.

Even the most unemotional of the Seattle Grace residents is not immune to this phenomenon. Cristina Yang, the resident who makes pre-pre-round rounds in order to cherry-pick the most interesting cases, fell in love with Preston Burke. I am doing my best to keep from going into a dangerous reverie extolling the virtues of Preston Burke. It could take all day. That voice. Those eyes. Those biceps. In essence, I'm saying, who can blame Cristina for that? I certainly don't. But he is most definitely the crack in Cristina's carefully constructed façade. What made Cristina cry? Finding out she was pregnant? No. Losing the pregnancy? No. Cristina cried when Burke came into her hospital room to check on her. Only he had truly found his way through her prickly exterior to her soft nougat center.

What I find fascinating about Cristina and Preston's relationship is the lack of information the two of them had about one another before they leapt into each other's arms and hearts. Cristina, who is clearly the kind of woman who hasn't taken a single step without contemplating whether it will take her further down the path that she's chosen, didn't have a clue about who Preston Burke really was. (I loved the moment on their first date when she said, shocked, "You don't eat red meat?" and he answered, "You do?" ["Let it Be," 2-8].)

75

No, the attending physicians at Seattle Grace are not immune to the travails of broken hearts, either. Cautious, careful, fussy Preston was blindsided by his feelings for Cristina just as much as she was by hers for him. There was McDreamy, of course, who I don't think expected to fall in love with Meredith any more than she expected to fall in love with him. Then there's Addison Montgomery-Shepherd, the woman who broke McDreamy's heart by dallying with his best friend, McSteamy.

It would have been so easy to paint Addison as an evil unfeeling bitch who cuckolded her sweet and sensitive husband, but one of the things I adore about *Grey's Anatomy* is that they rarely take the easy way out. Addison broke her own heart with her infidelity every bit as much as she broke Derek's. She was trying to use sex with another man to make herself feel better about a husband who was preoccupied and taking her for granted. It didn't work out so well. It may appear that this contradicts my thesis, but I don't believe so. Addison wasn't being slutty. She was being deceitful and, based on how hard she tried to get her husband back, she was deceiving herself as much as anyone else when she fell into bed with her husband's best friend.

While I don't believe that Addison contradicts my thesis that the doctors of Seattle Grace are safest when they indulge their bodies without involving their emotions, I do believe the exception that proves the rule is George O'Malley. George is, to me, the true heart of the show. He wanders the halls of Seattle Grace, seeing more than anyone gives him credit for with his sleepy puppy-dog eyes. George is the one Seattle Grace resident for whom sluttiness does not pay. When he slept with Olivia, the cute nurse who had been eyeing him for days and whom he liked but did not love, he got syphilis.

Everyone else on the show gives their hearts reluctantly or secretly or unknowingly. Cristina and Burke had to be secret for quite a while because of their respective positions in the hospital. Even after Burke "outed" them as a couple, their dance of intimacy was a supremely careful tap dance, not an exuberant dance of public love. Everyone may have known that Izzie and Alex went on a date and that the date didn't go well, but they saw Izzie's anger, not her hurt, and no one knew why Alex had gone all introspective and broody. While everyone else is shielding themselves and hiding their true feelings, George wears his heart pulsating on his sleeve for all the world to see. Everyone knew he had worshipped at Meredith's feet from the second he saw her.

It's hard to hand your heart to someone you have up on a pedestal, however. Heck, it's hard to get them to even look down and notice that you're offering it. Meredith knew George was there. She was even aware, on some level, that he was offering his love. One problem was that Meredith didn't want that from George. The other problem was that when things are up on a pedestal, you don't see them that clearly. George was more in love with the idea of Meredith than the complex, flawed, complicated woman that Meredith really was. No wonder things didn't go well when he finally slept with her.

Things didn't go all that well for Meredith at that moment, either. In the middle of having sex with George, she began to cry. But why? During the course of the show's two seasons, Meredith had had a fair amount of sex with men she didn't love, and she never cried in bed with them. The problem was, in my opinion, that Meredith did love George. She didn't love him the way he'd have liked her to love him, but her heart was open to him. She may have opened other body parts to all those other guys, but never her heart.

George literally poured his heart out to Meredith. He poured it out as if it were wine poured into a big cup and offered to her. Meredith knew what he was doing. It was exactly what she did when she turned to Derek and said, "Choose me." And she knew how much it hurt to offer yourself up only to be pushed away, even if the reasons for the rejection are noble. She tried to accept George, but she couldn't do it. She had already given her heart to Derek. Derek had given it back, but in the process he'd broken it.

Broken hearts eventually heal. They're never quite the same, but they're okay in the end. Maybe Meredith would be okay, too, if those guys had been enough. That's the real problem with sluttiness. A little may go a long way, but it never goes quite far enough. Lust is fun. It's a hot fudge sundae with a cherry on top, and like a hot fudge sundae it's momentarily satisfying but not long-run nourishing. Given a strict diet of ice cream, chocolate, and sprinkles, eventually you start to crave some solid meat and potatoes. You start to crave true love even though you know that once you give someone your heart you don't ever really get it back. If he breaks it, it may eventually mend, but it will never be quite the same, no matter how much slutty salve you slather on it.

Meredith tried desperately to protect her heart. She really did, but she couldn't. She couldn't protect anyone else's, either. Remember the episode where she had to hold a heart during a transplant surgery and realized after the surgery that her glove had ripped and her fingernail might have punctured the heart? She was literally holding someone's heart in her hands and she damaged it.

Interestingly, when George and Alex were stuck on an elevator with a patient and Preston Burke was giving them instructions on how to save the patient's life while they waited for the elevator to get unstuck, it was shy timid George, who had been dubbed "007" by the other residents, who had the nerve to stick his hand in the man's chest and plug the hole in his heart, not brash, brave, ballsy Alex. Alex froze up when the pressure was on, just like he did with Izzie.

77

That's gotta be a metaphor for something.

And here's what I think that metaphor is saying: No matter how many precautions you take, when you really care, no safety measure is enough to protect your tender, vulnerable heart. You can double-glove until the cows come home, but when someone else holds your heart in his or her hands, you may well get seriously hurt.

I should know. My own heart has been battered and bruised aplenty in my nearly four and a half decades. I've handed it to others only to have it handled carelessly, dropped reluctantly, or stomped on cruelly. It's scratched and stained and not nearly as resilient as it once was. So why do I keep trying? Why do I keep pulling my misshapen shattered treasure out of my chest and proffering it to others? Why not just walk away?

In Meredith's words, "I could quit, but here's the thing: I love the playing field" ("A Hard Day's Night," 1-1).

EILEEN RENDAHL was born in Dayton, Ohio, but moved when she was four and only remembers that she was born at the Good Samaritan Hospital across the street from Baskin Robbins because they sent her a coupon for a free ice cream cone every year until she was twelve. Eileen makes a point of remembering anything that has to do with ice cream. Or chocolate. Or champagne. She is the author of four novels, the most recent of which is *Un-Veiled*, the story of twin hairdressers who know too many of their clientele's secrets and not enough of their own.

Most of us try to keep some distance between our personal life and our work. But that assumes there's a difference; for the interns at Seattle Grace, their work is their life. They're so caught up in the drive to succeed as surgeons that everything else falls away. Janine Hiddlestone tells us what that means for their work, and for their relationships.

Janine Hiddlestone

DRAWING THE LINE

"Is this the strangest thing that's ever happened in your OR?" Meredith Grey asks Preston Burke as she tries not to move the hand she has inserted inside a patient's chest to stop him from bleeding and, more importantly, exploding. "I'd have to say that it is," Burke confirms. "Good," Meredith replies, "because I'm very competitive." Burke nods with approval: "All the best surgeons are" ("[As We Know It]," 2-17). While she is trying to lighten a very tense moment, she is nevertheless pleased to be the "most" something, even if it is the strangest or most dramatic moment in the OR. Here lies the central tenet of *Grey's Anatomy*: Competition is everything. Being a surgical intern is a life based on competition: getting through medical school, obtaining the internship, surviving it in order to become a surgeon (preferably, an eminent one).

Hospital dramas have been a mainstay on television since television's earliest years. The jaded roll their eyes at the mention of a new one, complaining that "there are so many," or something similar. And while there have been a considerable number, the tally pales in comparison with that of crime shows, or even soap operas. Perhaps hospital dramas cut a little close to home, since most people have been involved in at least one real-life hospital drama . . . but then again, who hasn't been impaled by a pole and hoped for George Clooney or Katherine Heigl to save them? There's as much wish fulfillment fantasy to hospital dramas as any other type of show, and their connection with painful realities does not appear to have damaged their appeal, with many showing respectable if not spectacular ratings throughout their lifetimes.

Despite the fact that all hospital shows invariably feature the overlap of life and death, love and loss—not to mention an impossibly good-looking staff—every show that has obtained ratings success has had a "hook" (sometimes more than one) in addition to its basic "hospital drama" concept. Ultimately, there needs to be more than cute doctors and cures to keep a show from cancellation. *Trapper John M.D.* used a beloved character from *M*A*S*H* to entice initial viewers, and kept them through generational conflict between John and the maverick but brilliant Gonzo; *Chicago Hope* had its eccentric staff and a singing surgeon; *ER* has its unique focus on the speed and urgency of the emergency room; and *House* has its grumpy, brilliant, and ethically flexible lead character—not unusual in itself, at least outside the U.S., but even in anti-hero-friendly England a drug-addled, cynical doctor who largely despises and avoids patients is unique. For *Grey's Anatomy*, the personal and professional lives of a group of surgical interns and their immediate superiors provide the underlying concept, but the "hook" is in the competitive miasma emanating from Seattle Grace Hospital and the resulting adrenaline seeping through every aspect of the characters' lives. Can they survive the challenging internship program, with its high failure rate? And, as importantly, can they survive each other?

If survival is the main aim of the surgical interns, then it seems obvious that competition would play a significant role in their lives. It is not that the idea of competition in work or play is in any way unusual. There is some degree of competitiveness to any endeavor—dating; getting the job, the promotion, the best bargain; even just getting a parking spot within hiking distance two days before Christmas. However, for the surgical interns on *Grey's Anatomy*, the competitive level is more like obtaining prime advertising space for the Super Bowl, which is, of course, much more competitive than the game itself. And this competition is a matter of life and death, not only for the patients, but for the doctors themselves, because as intern Alex Karev reminds us, surgery is less a career choice than a calling: Failure is not an option.

There is a certain arrogance in these characters' attitude toward their professions and their place in the world. Their job is more important than everyone else's, and everyone else. It is not enough to compete with each other; they also compete with everyone else in their lives. Even George O'Malley, the "nice guy" of the show and by far the least arrogant of the group, made it clear to his family (during a Thanksgiving turkey-hunting trip) that he considered their jobs and lives to be much less important than his own ("Thanks for the Memories," 2-9). This point is belabored at regular intervals, so much so that it is difficult to know whether the writers are explaining it or criticizing it—or perhaps a mixture of both. This is not to suggest that the job of surgeons is not an important one, deserving of respect, but the emphasis put on their elevated status can become a little wearing. And ultimately, it is not social status but surgery itself that brings out the most competitive aspects of the interns' personalities.

The ruthlessness of the competition was obvious from the first episode. Even nerves and a dreaded fear of their resident, "the Nazi," did not prevent their attempts to secure a surgery within hours of their arrival. When George, who was the unexpected recipient of the first honors, stepped into the OR, he was faced not only with the specter of the many experienced participants surrounding him, but also a gallery of his peers, watching him from behind the glass above him. They placed bets and heckled, practices that became common. It was like a form of blood sport, like ice hockey or football watched from a private box. The other interns were spectators, but also alternates, who could be called out on to the field of play anytime. Every match is a final; even the most mundane procedure is a risk. Their envy of George quickly abated when the appendectomy went wrong. Although it was not his fault, he temporarily became a pariah, as well as an object of ridicule, dubbed "007." Despite his having the first surgery, his colleagues felt able to reassert their place in the scheme of things through George's failure.

The first hospital shift also saw the emergence of the friendship and rivalry between Meredith and the brilliant but seemingly emotionless Cristina Yang. When Derek Shepherd tasked the interns with helping to make a difficult diagnosis in exchange for a place on the surgical team,

81

Meredith and Cristina banded together, recognizing a common drive and intelligence. Meredith told Cristina that she could have the surgery if they succeeded, as Meredith was anxious to demonstrate her ability and commitment to the internship after the humiliation of discovering that Shepherd had been her anonymous one-night stand from the previous evening. However, when the interns' diagnosis proved to be correct, Meredith betrayed Cristina by taking the surgery. However, what appeared to infuriate Cristina more were Meredith's attempts to apologize: "You know you did a cut-throat thing. Deal with it. Don't come to me for absolution. You want to be a shark. Be a shark" ("A Hard Day's Night," 1-1).

The competition is not just for surgery itself, but also the most unusual or challenging surgeries. The interns vie for the most likely surgical cases, and then further for the most interesting and complex ones. This leads, on occasion, to a seemingly callous disregard for the individual patients. And attempts to pick and choose cases can backfire. Cristina's pre-rounds discovery of a prickly but much loved retired scrub nurse with cancer, whom Cristina believed would require a rare "wipple" surgery, ended up chaining her to a case where surgery had already been decided against ("No Man's Land," 1-4). Alex managed to charm his way into the surgery of a woman with a grotesquely huge tumor by sweet-talking the patient, but she later requested he be taken off her case when she found out his true feelings about her situation ("If Tomorrow Never Comes," 1-6). While each of these resulted in a "lesson" in humility and humanity for the intern involved, it did little to deter either one of them in the future: The allure of diagnosing a "pregnant" man convinced Cristina, with Izzie, to poach him from another service ("Something to Talk About," 2-7). Cristina lost her place on a train crash victim's surgical team when Alex went behind her back, tracking down a missing leg himself though he knew she was searching for it, and took her place ("Into You Like a Train," 2-6). Surgery, after all, is the reason the interns are there; delivering lab results or being stuck in the emergency room is treated with disdain.

It is easy to be critical of this behavior. But even as the resident and attending surgeons berate them for their actions, they do little to discourage it because it is seen as part of the learning process. The residents' and attendings' seniority also does not prevent them from occasionally playing

82

the game themselves. This most commonly manifests in the rivalry between Burke and Shepherd, but we see it also with Bailey, the doctor with the most developed moral compass. Pregnant and working on Thanksgiving, she was asked by Meredith why she had volunteered to be there. Her reply was that she needed to take all the opportunities that she could with the baby coming. Besides which, the most interesting cases, the ones resulting in the most surgeries, came through that day because of "too much family time": "The stupidity of the human race, Grey. Be thankful for it" ("Thanks for the Memories," 2-9). Moreover, berating her interns for "stealing" the "pregnant" man was simply lip service; she also congratulated them for their find, because it reflected well on her. Clearly, the competition does not end with the internship.

Neither does the competitive atmosphere begin and end at the hospital door. In the second episode, Meredith announced that she was "drawing the line" ("The First Cut is the Deepest," 1-2) between her personal and professional lives, but despite this decision soon realized that a separation of the two was impossible. Their jobs are so all-consuming that their professional lives do not just overlap into their personal lives, they are completely integrated. In their race to the top of their professions, the interns have all attempted to outrun aspects of their past—usually something to do with their families—but as everyone learns, you can never run far enough or fast enough. For no one is this more accurate than Meredith herself: Her mother is a famous surgeon who refused to support her daughter's career choice, apparently believing her not up to the task. Meredith has had to deal with the resentment of her fellow interns, who believe her mother's influence will result in special treatment, and superiors who compare her abilities with her mother's. The paradox is that her mother is in a nursing home just a few miles away, suffering from early onset Alzheimer's—a burden Meredith must carry alone. Moreover, the situation locks her relationship with her mother into her childhood, where she is more of a nuisance than a beloved child. She is therefore left to compete not only with her mother the surgeon, whom only Meredith is aware no longer exists, but also for her mother's approval, which she will never obtain.

It was at least partly because of this that Meredith made her decision to "draw the line." The desire to keep her personal life private seems sensible: How can you be friends with people with whom you must compete so fiercely? She was also half-heartedly attempting to break off a burgeoning affair with her boss, a relationship that was likely only to increase the envy of her colleagues. This was clearly articulated by Meredith in the third episode:

> We live out our lives on the surgical unit. Seven days a week, fourteen hours a day. We're together more than we're apart. After a while the ways of residency become the ways of life.
>
> Number one. Always keep score.
>
> Number two. Do whatever you can to outsmart the other guy.
>
> Number three. Don't make friends with the enemy.
> ("Winning a Battle, Losing the War," 1-3)

Nevertheless, she soon realized that she had little choice other than to allow her life to intermesh with her colleagues', despite the competition. As an intern, there is no time or room in her life for people outside the hospital. As her fellow intern and housemate Izzie Stevens discovered, it is very difficult to sustain a relationship with someone who does not understand or accept that the job comes first. Izzie made this clear when her hockey player boyfriend came to visit and she sabotaged the visit (partly subconsciously) by throwing a party and filling the house with people who worked at the hospital while staying at work herself ("Shake Your Groove Thing," 1-5). When confronted by the boyfriend, she explained that he was no longer her first priority. Although he tried to tell her that he understood, and just wanted to be with her when she was available, Izzie told him that it was the people at the party who understood what her life entailed now, even if they did not know her well. Understandably, he left, getting the message more clearly than Izzie intended.

While close relationships with other hospital staff are treated as inevitable, interns are taught not to become too personally involved with their patients—therefore encouraging them not to see too far past the surgeries themselves. Patients are often referred to not by name but by medical ailment. This approach does have some grounding in logic, as becoming too invested can be dangerous for the surgeon *and* the patient. All the interns have found themselves in this position at least once, some of them more often than others. Surgical resident Addison Montgomery-Shepherd decided to try to teach Izzie, one of the worst offenders, a lesson involving a dying premature baby, and by the time the cruel exercise was complete, the baby was dead and Izzie's spirit was broken ("Owner of a Lonely Heart," 2-11). However, while this lesson may have worked on other interns (Addison implies that it did on her, when she was an intern), it apparently did not take with Izzie, as seen most painfully in her relationship with heart patient Denny Duquette. Finding a middle ground between callous indifference and deep emotional investment proves to be one of the most challenging tasks for the interns, both with their patients and in their personal relationships. Meredith recognized this issue early on in her attempts to disconnect herself by drawing lines:

> At some point you have to make a decision. Boundaries don't keep other people out. They fence you in. Life is messy. That's how we're made. So you can waste your life drawing lines. Or you can live your life crossing them. ("The First Cut is the Deepest," 1-2)

But despite her decision to abandon line-drawing, it soon became obvious that life without them is no easier. For the most part, the middle ground has remained unattainable: The extremes may be dangerous, but they are also an unavoidable part of the game.

The adrenaline high of surgery—the intensity it produces, which leads to such extremes—is an integral component of the plot. After Meredith's first surgery, and a forty-eight-hour shift, Meredith was both stunned and invigorated. "That was amazing," she told Shepherd. "That was such a high. I don't know why anybody does drugs" ("A Hard Day's Night," 1-1). However, just as drugs are addictive, so is the adrenaline rush. Surgeons tend to be risk takers (on television, at least), whether in war zones or the rarified damp air of Seattle. In *Grey's Anatomy*, the high adrenaline creates an unmistakable sexual charge in the atmosphere. Cristina and Burke began a sexual relationship after speaking less than a dozen words to each other but working together on a couple of particularly tense cases ("If Tomorrow Never Comes," 1-6). Meredith and Shepherd fooled around, after a drama-filled day, in a car right outside a party at which hospital staff were present—and the worst possible scenario, Bailey was an unwilling witness ("Shake Your Groove Thing," 1-5). Izzie and Alex had four "encounters" during a Code Black at the hospital, and Alex has been known to take "breaks" with nurses in between surgeries ("It's the End of the World," 2-16). This is apparently nothing new, as suggested by the revelation that Meredith's mother, Ellis, conducted a torrid extramarital affair at the hospital with the current Chief back when they were both residents ("Make Me Lose Control," 2-3).

While sexual relationships with colleagues can clearly cause problems, sometimes those "difficulties" are more physical in nature. When George contracted syphilis from a sexual encounter (apparently his first in some time), he was faced with the indignity of being examined, treated, and made fun of by his fellow interns ("Who's Zoomin' Who?," 1-9). Worse, though, he discovered that his girlfriend (an ER nurse) had contracted it from Alex, and that there was a mini-epidemic among the hospital staff, which prompted the Chief to force all staff into a safe-sex class. However disquieting the situation, it underscored the fact that fraternizing between colleagues is hardly unusual.

86

Alex was not fazed by his encounter with syphilis, but was mortified by his inability to function sexually with Izzie in the early stages of their relationship (obviously before the Code Black encounters). As the problem turned out to be psychological, two reasons can be suggested to explain the situation. The first is that he truly cares for Izzie, a unique concept for him. The other is that it is about competition. Alex had just found out he'd failed part of his board exam, had made some mistakes on the job, and would be dropped from the program if he failed his retest. In the context of his setbacks, Izzie—or the idea of her—suddenly became threatening, and he turned to ex-girlfriend Olivia to restore his confidence ("Much Too Much," 2-10). For Alex, Olivia is "just" a nurse, and therefore not part of the competition. (Of course, it did nothing to assist his relationship with Izzie.)

To be fair, the cloud of sexual energy wafting over Seattle Grace Hospital is not only the result of its horny surgeons. Sometimes it's brought in by the patients. One man with prostate cancer refused to be treated by Izzie after recognizing her as an underwear model he had admired in a magazine because he did not want her to be privy to the procedure that would likely make him impotent. Although initially embarrassed and insulted, it was Izzie who salvaged the patient's "manhood" when she stood up to a dismissive surgeon to compel him to save the man's viable nerves and therefore sexual ability ("No Man's Land," 1-4). In a more humorous situation, after Shepherd had prescribed watching porn as a pain killer to a patient allergic to other methods, a power outage found an initially disgusted Cristina telling a tale of "naughty nurses"—with alarming proficiency—to help the patient relax ("Bring the Pain," 2-5). In another episode, Meredith's latest one-night stand appeared at the hospital the morning after with a persistent erection that ended up requiring brain surgery (obviously). Meredith was taunted all day for "breaking his penis," a Freudian image if ever there was one ("Much Too Much," 2-10). Similarly, a woman with regular involuntary orgasms ("It's not exactly something you want to cure is it?") requires assistance ("Yesterday," 2-18), while elsewhere in the hospital the surgeons had to remove a fork from the neck of another woman after a seizure caused her to lock her jaw on her husband's . . . oh, never mind—you get the idea ("Band-Aid Covers the Bullet Hole," 2-20).

Although it is difficult to underestimate the symbolic impact of the above cases, none is as startling as the severed penis in the first season ("The First Cut is the Deepest," 1-2). When a woman was brought in unconscious after being brutally attacked, an attempt to save her in the OR uncovered the fact that she had wreaked her revenge on her assailant by biting off his penis. The "evidence" had to be passed on to the police, of course, and protocol demanded that one of the staff involved in the operation—Meredith, in this case—retain custody of the body part until it was officially handed over. She therefore had to spend the day carrying the penis around in a cooler box, making her the focus of curiosity from some and trepidation from others. Against the odds, the attacked woman survived intact, while her attacker was caught, thanks to her, no longer intact. This storyline introduced a recurring theme: emasculation and the restoration of control.

While the example of the attempted rape victim and her attacker was far from subtle—the victim regained control of her body and her destiny by her actions and permanently removed the control of her attacker through his emasculation—it is that lack of subtlety that draws attention to the theme's recurrence. George felt emasculated by housemates Meredith and Izzie when they behaved in a "sisterly" fashion toward him, particularly since he was in love with Meredith ("No Man's Land," 1-4). Alex felt emasculated by not only his sexual problems, but also his professional failings—and attempted to regain his own sense of control by sleeping with Olivia. Burke was affronted by Cristina's inability to communicate with him on a personal level—and her inability to stay awake during sex ("Damage Case," 2-24). Metaphorical emasculation is not reserved only for the male characters, as the issue of control is just as significant for the women. Meredith's "line" was an attempt at control, as were her one-night stands. For Cristina, her emotional wall and seemingly selfish exterior are control mechanisms, as are Izzie's attempts at creating the "perfect" familial atmosphere: her obsessive baking, her affection for the holidays, and strong attachments to others. For Bailey, it is her "Nazi" persona, as demonstrated after her maternity leave when she felt that people saw her differently because she was a mother and respected (feared?) her less ("The Name of the Game," 2-22). And while the sexual liaisons among the staff can be seen as an extension of the high adrenaline "sport" of surgery, they can sometimes also be a source of comfort—and control—when the game is lost. This can, of course, have catastrophic results at times: Meredith and Dr. McDreamy; Meredith and George; Meredith and "broken penis guy"; Cristina's pregnancy; and everyone's syphilis. Luckily, the repercussions keep the story interesting.

When competition and sex intertwine in *Grey's Anatomy*, the result of that combination is that extra "edginess" that is such an important part of the show's success. One of the challenges writers of hospital dramas face is not allowing their show to become mired in the daily life and death struggles and troubled relationships of the surgeons. Relying on the usual "will they, or won't they?" romantic storyline that has alternately promoted and haunted almost every drama and sitcom in recent memory isn't enough (if they get together, the fans will lose interest: If they don't get together, the fans will lose interest); a show needs something more. *ER*, the longest-running of the recent crop of hospital dramas, has attempted to retain its edge through "special events" that do not shy from making political statements, and although the show has retained its quality, it has nevertheless suffered a gradual decline in its ratings (Keveney). Viewers are always looking for something new. The controversial decision by the writers of *Grey's Anatomy* to give "nice guy" George (and half the staff) syphilis was motivated in part by the fact that, as writers Gabrielle Stanton and Harry Werksman noted on the writers' blog, "*ER* hasn't done it."

The competition to keep a show on the air is a fierce one. The contest is sometimes underhanded, and the field is littered with the bodies of both the woeful and the talented that have failed to capture an audience among viewers with increasingly short attention spans. Sex and controversy help, but even they become passé without more to hold viewers' attention. Ultimately, the irony is that *Grey's Anatomy's* emphasis on competition is what has catapulted it above its sister medical dramas to win its own competition: the ratings game.

To paraphrase Meredith, "Is this the strangest thing that has ever happened on your television?" Probably not, but it's certainly a very competitive contender.

JANINE HIDDLESTONE is a lecturer and tutor in politics, history, and communications at James Cook University in Australia. She has a Ph.D. in political history and has published on the place of war in culture and history, and how pop culture became the centerpiece of so much of the public's understanding—and misunderstanding—of events. She has explored the influence of technology on pop culture, and vice versa, and its pedagogical uses in encouraging students to develop an interest in political and historical issues. She has also attained infamy among her colleagues as a pop culture tragic.

REFERENCES

Keveney, Bill. "*ER* ratings bleed is nothing too traumatic." *U.S.A. Today*: 10 Nov. 2004. <http://usatoday.com/life/television/news/2004-11-10-er-main_x.htm>

Rhimes, Shonda. *Frequently Asked Questions* [Interview with Shonda Rhimes]. June 2006. <http://abc.go.com/primetime/greysanatomy/faq.html>

Stanton, Gabrielle and Harry Werksman. "Harry and Gabrielle on Syphilis!" *Grey Matter*. 3 Aug. 2006. <http://www.greyswriters.com/>

Looking for a successful career in surgery? Here's a tip: Figure out what the doctors at Seattle Grace would do—and do the opposite.

Erin Dailey

BRUSHING UP ON YOUR BEDSIDE MANNER

WHAT WE'VE LEARNED FROM THE DELIGHTFUL DOCS AT SEATTLE MEMORIAL GRACE HOLY SISTER CATHEDRAL HOSPITAL

Tending to the sick. Helping those in need. Saving lives. It's all part and parcel of being a doctor. You want to touch people, heal them, make their worlds a little brighter with the knowledge that their doctor really, truly cares about them.

But how can you do all this without it getting in the way of your active social life? Do you really have to pay attention to the patients? Because sometimes that part of the job kind of sucks. When do you get to have fun? When do the big bucks start rolling in? Who's the new attending and what's his number, because sister's gettin' antsy. . . .

If these are questions you're asking yourself as you enter into the challenging world of make-believe medicine, don't worry—the answers are within reach. And, luckily, they're delivered by the toothsome doctors and doctresses of Seattle Grace Hospital. Or is it Seattle Memorial Grace Hospital? Or Seattle Grace Holy Virgin Cathedral Memorial Hot DAMN That New Intern Is FIIIIIINE Hospital? Oh, who cares? We're too busy learning life lessons along with the interns and watching Derek and Meredith do their never-ending dating dance to bother with silly things like hospital names!

Somehow, our favorite interns and their supervisors manage to care for their various patients while maintaining friendships and romances with each other that the average human being with a typical nine-to-five job couldn't handle with a personal assistant and a staff of ten for support. And on top of this interpersonal multi-tasking, they also throw in some valuable "learning-from-our-patients'-ailments-and-situations" internal monologuing that must occur in the one corner of their brains that isn't used for healing the sick, directing scalpels, or making out with their co-workers.

How in the hell do they do all this? We can barely balance our checkbooks, let alone our business and personal lives.

Maybe it's time we looked to the interns and the attendings for the answers we seek. Even if we don't all want to become imaginary doctors, their well-worn advice can come in handy.

Especially if you start dating your hot boss with the fabulously floppy hair.

For ease of use, these tips have been divided into four sections: Patient Care, Sex and Love, Interoffice Interpersonal Interrelations (a.k.a. Work Relationships), and Self-Improvement.

Strap yourself to a banana bag and get reading, people! There are patients to save and inappropriate love affairs to conduct!

HOW TO CARE FOR PATIENTS (WITHOUT REALLY TRYING)

People go to doctors for many reasons, but most of them just want their shit fixed. It's like going to the garage for a tune-up: Get me in, get me out, and get me back on the road. The last thing people want to hear from their doctor is how their life choices are affecting their health. Too bad, really, because half the time, their life choices really suck and you have to tell them anyway.

Here are a few things to keep in mind as you treat your patients:

DO:

Try and talk to your patients like they're human. Why? Well, because they are. Duh. Just because you're too busy thinking about that brain you want to stick your scalpels into after lunch doesn't mean you should speed through your diagnoses and leave your patients swimming in indecipherable medical jargon until they're drowning in it and gasping for air. Rattling off a bunch of scary words that end in "itis" and "ancer" without even considering that the patient might not understand what you're saying is never a good idea. And doing it in a really flat, emotionless voice is even worse. What sort of whack-ass Hippocratic Oath are you operating under, anyway? The "The-More-You-Can-Confuse-and-Bewilder-Your-Patients-the-Better" version? Because that's just not right, dude. Sure, telling your patients the truth is fine, and, really, recommended, but at least try to make sure you're delivering it with an eye toward not totally freaking them out. The most important thing to remember is that, even though you practiced on cadavers during medical school, those people in front of you in the beds are NOT DEAD YET. If it helps, pretend your patients are just reanimated cadavers. And if they ask you why you're giggling, just tell them you've had one too many hits of ether. They love that. Especially right before they go into surgery.

DON'T:
Get too involved with your patients. They're not your family, so don't treat them as such. Even if they ARE your family, don't get too involved with them. Maintain a professional, disinterested distance from your patients, and then you won't have to deal with all their silly "worries" and "second opinions" and stuff like that. Okay, not really. You can get close to your patients, just don't get *too* close. Like, don't sleep with them. And try not to tell them any personal information. They'll only use it against you. Oh, and it's particularly important that you don't fall in love with your patients. WE MEAN IT. Falling in love with patients is really super-duper against the rules here, especially if they're likely to die. If they're likely to die, this will only end in heartache. And death. And a funeral. Which is never as fun as the falling in love part so, just, you know, don't do it.

DON'T:
Underestimate the power of honesty. When a patient isn't following your recommendation to terminate a pregnancy so that she can get chemo and possibly live a few more years, by all means, tell her what you think. You'll probably make her feel like shit, but at least you'll have been honest. Sometimes people need to hear honesty from doctors; it's

93

so rare that a patient can get a straight answer from her doctors that maybe, just maybe, you'll wind up helping her. You also might wind up sounding like a complete bitch and your patient will hate you, but at least she'll know she got a dead-on straightforward honest answer, and how often can a patient say that? Just make sure you're not using your own personal problems to fuel your honesty moments; nobody likes a sore loser. Especially when the sore loser in question is prescribing medication and, you know, sticking a scalpel into flesh. Honesty is all well and good, but if you're just trying to come to terms with some personal shit you're dealing with, leave the honesty at the door. And then go get yourself a Slushie, because there's nothing a little brain freeze can't fix.

SEX AND THE SINGLE DOCTOR

Any office environment can lend itself to moments of inappropriate sexual conduct. Hello, anyone ever been to a holiday office party, like, ever? Because, yeah. Three glasses of champagne and suddenly you and the security guard are doing the horizontal mambo up against the copy machine.

But in the case of doctors, mixing business with pleasure, as it were, can lead to some sticky situations. And by "sticky situation," we mean, "while arguing about your exes your patient goes into cardiac arrest and you have to perform CPR on him/her while your attending boyfriend looks on and wonders how many lovers you've had before him." Or something like that.

Look. Sex is going to happen. Especially if you're with a bunch of hot doctors 24/7. Just make sure you follow a couple of guidelines and you'll come out smiling. Especially if orgasms are involved.

DO:
Avoid having sex with every last person you can get your hands on, especially if one of them happens to be your boss. We cannot stress this enough: It's incredibly important for you NOT to sleep with your superiors, because doing so may ruin your career and therefore your life. It's not enough that you have to remember billions of medical terms and cures and be able to spew them out at a moment's notice, or that every time you touch a patient, you worry that you run the risk of

killing him or her because you're just a stupid intern—do you also want to be worrying that your affair with your boss could kill your future plans? There are twenty-four hours in the day, people. Put them to good use by avoiding the well-worn trap of sleeping with inappropriate people in inappropriate places at inappropriate times. Don't you have anything better to do with your time? Like, um, SAVE LIVES? Yes, the attending surgeon is adorable and the way he makes his eyes crinkle when he smiles at you is nearly irresistible. RESIST IT. Put on an eye mask whenever he's in range! Lock yourself in a supply closet! (But make sure one of the other interns isn't in there having sex with HER [or his] boss before you do.) You have the rest of your life to have sex with the wrong person; use your time on the floor to do good with something other than your sexual organs.

DO:
Find out if the person you're sleeping with has a secret spouse tucked away somewhere. When he keeps getting mysterious cell phone calls that he won't answer and refuses to tell you what his favorite color is or how many siblings he has or even IF HE HAS A DAMN HOUSE, you must walk away. WALK AWAY. These are all signs. Signs that the person you're sleeping with is a lying asshole who not only has a SPOUSE, but said spouse is now working at the very same hospital YOU BOTH WORK AT. Don't cry. Don't beg. Don't crawl. Just walk the hell away. You'll feel better about yourself in the long run. And even if you don't, you'll at least be able to get yourself a Slushie on the way.

DON'T:
Have sex with that intern who thinks he's God's gift to women. Just don't. Unless you WANT every last STD on the face of the planet all up in your business.

DO:
Avoid punching the lights out of anyone who even thinks of coming near your new intern girlfriend. Sure, your estranged wife is in town and you might be toying with the idea of getting back together with her, but that doesn't mean you need to trumpet your feelings about your intern

95

girlfriend all over the damn hospital, dude! And, really, why in the hell do you still care about that little intern you're jerking around on a long chain? YOU broke up with HER and yet, YET, you're still concerned about whom she sleeps with. Shouldn't this tell you something? Yes. Yes, it should. And what it should tell you is that you love HER and not your EX (no matter how awesome your ex may be). Note: This method of showing your affection toward your new girlfriend may very well alienate you from her affections and, possibly, make your estranged wife want to take a hit out on your life. We're just warning you.

DON'T:
Move in with that resident you're screwing. You can think about it all you want, you can think he is sweet and powerful and really good in the sack. You can think about all these things FROM YOUR OWN APARTMENT. Because if you move in with him, you're just going to gross him out with your eating in bed and spitting in the sink and crazy frugging in the living room, and all the while, your control freak boyfriend will think you're not opening yourself up for love and being cagey about your past and your dreams and blah blah blah whatever and you should just save yourself the trouble and STAY AT HOME. You can still see him every night of the week; just make sure you ain't seeing him at every breakfast, too.

DO:
Start dating that hot veterinarian with all the facial hair. For one thing, he's hot. For another, he's hot. For yet another, he seems to think all your weird relationship issues and phobias are adorable. For yet ANOTHER, he is NOT your boss. Also? Did we mention the hot part?

DON'T:
Go after your almost-ex-husband at his new place of work unless you want to be surprised by his new girlfriend and a bunch of interns who hate you just because you want to reclaim your almost-ex even though he kind of might sort of hate you a lot. Do yourself a favor and stay in New York. This is not a reflection on you as a person, you understand; we're sure you're very nice and have many lovely qualities. But you're messing with our notions of true love and shit and we hate that.

DO:

Use protection when having sex. We can't even believe that, in this day and age, we have to say something like this, but, um, there's a chance that you'll get syphilis or, um, pregnant if you don't. And yet, surprisingly, a great number of interns and even ATTENDINGS neglect to do this. Yeah. We know. Don't even get us started. Go on the Pill, get an IUD, get a sponge, get a vasectomy, have your tubes tied, buy stock in Trojan. Just get something and USE IT, okay? Seriously. And if you use condoms, make sure they're not glow-in-the-dark, because those are just stupid and might get you laughed out of bed. No, really. REALLY.

DON'T:

Forget what we said about that fellow intern of yours with the faulty naughty parts. He'll make you all itchy in places where you really don't want to be. Fine. Don't listen to us. But make sure you wear a condom. Or ten. Hell, wear full body armor—this dude's nasty.

YOU ARE THE WIND BENEATH MY STANDARD-ISSUE STETHOSCOPE

Without getting too maudlin on your asses, we'd just like to say that without your friends, you are nothing. It's true. On those days when your boyfriend/girlfriend refuses to speak to you for no reason, your boss forces you to do menial tasks because he/she apparently just doesn't like you anymore, and the last three patients you treated either kicked the bucket or lapsed into comas, the only people you can turn to are your friends. They lift you up when you're down, bring you back to earth when you get too lofty, and offer you a shoulder to cry on even as they manage to tell you that you're totally in the wrong and the shoulder is only being offered reluctantly because, hi, this is all your fault.

That being said, it's probably a really good idea not to alienate or hurt your friends because, at the end of the day, they're all you've got, baby.

DO:

Tell your Nosy Parker friend to stop nosing into your business and keep on walking. You know she means well and everything, but you get plenty of unwanted advice from other interns and your bosses and even your boss that you're sleeping with (even though we told you not to); you don't need any more from her. She might say she's only trying to be helpful, but what she's really being is nosy, and it's annoying as hell. Also? She's kind of being judgmental, which is SO uncalled for, especially when you're dealing with one-night stands, alcohol abuse problems, a couple of boyfriends, a scary girlfriend, anger-management issues, or a penchant for giving people syphilis. Oh, and people who live in glass muffin-filled houses shouldn't throw stones; she's clearly dealing with her own damn issues, and when she has them, you're always totally supportive of her and never judge her and now that she's lost her fiancé, maybe she'll knock it off with the whole "What are you DOING?" bullshit she's been so busy handing out since you first met her. The next time she tries to nose in on your shit, just tell her you need more muffins. That'll shut her up, but quick.

DO:

Remove yourself from the remote possibility that you will sleep with that puppy-eyed intern you live with. He is your friend and you're messing with his head enough as it is, so sleeping with him just because he says he loves you is a really BAD idea. Really? Are you really that person? Do you want to be known as the "chick who sleeps with guys just because they say they love her"? Because that is just sad, baby. Just . . . sad. Don't do it. Do you need us to draw you a map? BECAUSE WE WILL.

DO:

Stop being a big ol' Nosy Parker to all your friends. You're a beautiful, warm, considerate human being; you don't need to get all up in your buddies' business! All you're doing is making people hate and resent you, and you don't deserve that. Enough with the offering up of the uninvited opinions and the inserting yourself into every conversation and the bossy judgmental know-it-all crap. Your friends don't really care what you think (okay, some of them do, but still) and they may even tell you to fuck off and die, and that can't possibly be something you want to endure. Especially when your so-called "advice" makes them feel like a foot-tall leper with a horned tail. Get down off your high-horse, punkin. You don't look any prettier up there than you do down here, okay?

DO:

Try not lusting after your friends. There's a great chance that at least one of them is out of your league, but even if she were in your league, you really should pick someone else to lust after. And, for God's sake, don't MOVE IN WITH the object of your lust. You can tell yourself you just need someplace to stay other than your childhood bedroom at home (really? No, REALLY?) and that this living situation is going to be totally normal and not awkward at all, BUT YOU WILL BE WRONG. You are telling yourself LIES. You lust after your roommate and now you live with her and she tells you all about her boy problems and all you can do is sulk over the fact that she doesn't have boy problems with YOU and this is not a healthy way to live, dude. And talking about her incessantly to anyone who will listen isn't doing you any favors, either. Even deaf people in the vicinity are desperately signing at you to shut the hell up. You need to wake up, get out of that house, and grow a pair. Of course, once you do, you'll probably hook up with a crazy bitch who lives in the hospital basement and pees with the door open and seems to go from zero to commitment in two-point-five seconds, but at least you won't still be lusting after your damn roommate. Good luck, man. You're going to need it.

99

PHYSICIAN, HEAL THYSELF

A healthy doctor is a good doctor. And by "healthy" we are clearly talking about "mental health," because no one really cares if you've got a head cold or the syph. This is why we suggest that you do a little internal inventory of your problems and issues and DEAL with them rather than IGNORE them. How can you concentrate on the patient before you if all you're doing is thinking about your own messed-up little mental universe? It's time to turn that stethoscope around and make a few self-diagnoses.

Your patients will thank you for it. (And so will we, because DAMN do you have some serious issues.)

DO:

Stop turning everything back around so that it's alllll about you. What in the HELL are you doing? You have patients and they have needs. Nine times out of ten, their needs have LITERALLY NOTHING TO DO

WITH YOU. Look at what you're doing to yourself and your patients, here. Patient has unnecessary gastric bypass surgery? That's about you and your mommy issues. Two patients impaled by a pole and stuck together? Clearly, that's a metaphor for your bad relationships and why you're currently suffering through YET ANOTHER ONE. One of your fellow interns is pregnant? Obviously, that's a warning sign about what could happen to YOU if you keep sleeping with your boss. Dude. We all appreciate that patients can make us contemplate our own place in the world, but seriously. You are a DOCTOR. There are other people on this planet besides you. And the boss you keep sleeping with. And his ex. Sorry. We lost focus there for a second. There are most certainly OTHER PEOPLE you have to worry about. Try paying attention to them without bringing it back around to you. For a change.

DON'T:
Forget you're a man, man! (If, indeed, you are a man—there are some among us who are dangerously close to crossing over into girl-land. We're not naming any names, but his initials are George.) Look, this is the new millennium. The days of women crying and weeping over you not calling them or constantly asking for definitions of your bur-geoning relationship are over, dude. (Except in the case of someone among our ranks who just never seems to get enough of the old Q&A. Again, we'll change names to protect the innocent, *Meredith*.) The odds are more likely that she'll grab you and throw you in a storage closet and rip your clothes off and YOU'LL be the one requesting rela-tionship clarification. If, for whatever reason, the woman in your life doesn't ask questions, just wants to have sex all the time, and seems to have little or no interest in your personal life OR your past, then by all means, GO WITH IT. Thaaaat's right. Don't demand answers, don't turn her away; don't, in short, start ACTING LIKE A GIRL. Isn't it enough that you're getting laid? Just enjoy it. You'll thank us later.

DO:
Stop drinking. Not all the time, OBVIOUSLY. But just stop drinking right after your shift; you never know when you'll be called back. And stop drinking before your shift. That's . . . just not right. There's not a single

person with health insurance out there who wants a doctor who reeks of tequila. Well, maybe there's a person or two who would welcome a doctor who smells like a stein of beer, but that person or two is probably an idiot who's trying to find a reason to sue a hospital for MALPRACTICE. Look. As much as you might think it's necessary to drink in order to erase all your damn relationship problems, we are here to tell you: They. Will. Never. Go. Away. No matter how much you drink. You will still have to deal with them. Yes, the alcohol will make dealing with them so much easier. We're career alcoholics ourselves. We understand this. But if you drink to hide your pain, your pain will eventually show up as a patient with a bad heart or a person with a big pole or tree driven through his or her chest and then you'll have to think, "Would a drink help right here? Because I'm not sure it really would. God, I want a beer. But I have to deal with my PATIENT now. I'll . . . dammit. I'll drink ON THE WEEKEND WHEN I'M SUPPOSED TO." Just . . . keep the drinking to a minimum, okay? Insurance doesn't pay for drunken eejits.

DON'T:

Keep baking and cooking and trying to recapture a childhood never had. You can try to cook that turkey dinner for all your intern friends on Thanksgiving, you can over-decorate the house in tinsel and lights for Christmas, you can even try to replicate your mother's bizarre cupcake recipe that strangely resembles a Hostess cupcake, but you will never ever EVER erase the fact that you grew up in a trailer park. A sad childhood doesn't make you a bad person, and all the cupcakes in the world aren't going to make your depressing past disappear. Just remember that you're a delightful person and a good doctor and you need to stop drowning yourself in the kitchen and just go ahead and go to a damn NASCAR race and learn to love yourself. But can we have a couple cookies for the road first? Those things are AWESOME.

DON'T:

Beat yourself up too much for your mistakes. You're human. Just like your patients. You're bound to make mistakes. But as a doctor, or as a future doctor, you really need to learn from them. How wonderful will your medical career be if you never learn that judging your patients based on your own moral backbone will only alienate them and possibly land you in a hefty malpractice suit? What kind of doctor will you be if you never understand that life is precious and that, when you hold it in your hands, you're not a god, you're just a temporary caretaker? How will you feel, years from now, if you never stopped for a moment to appreciate just what an amazing thing it is to be one of the few people on the planet who can actually save a life? You need to mess up as much as possible and not forget about it when you do. Because, someday, you're going to be faced with the same problems you've screwed up on in the past and you're actually going to know what to do right. Just don't make the same mistake twice. Life ain't a dress rehearsal, dude.

DO:

. . . Yourself a favor and stop messing around with your personal life and start paying attention to your medical career. Sure, all that personal life stuff is fun and even more fun to WATCH, but at some point, you're going to have to cut someone open and save a life and it would be a really good idea if you, you know, KNEW WHAT YOU WERE DOING.

But keep sleeping with your boss, just in case that doesn't work out for you.

ERIN DAILEY is a freelance writer and Web designer who also happens to have the best damn day job in the world. She moved to New York City last year and would like you to know that she's already becoming one of those insufferable New Yorkers who thinks that no place else in the world compares to the Big Apple. Yes, she's already totally annoying. When she's not pretending that she's super cool, she covers the TV show *Heroes* on Television Without Pity (www.televisionwithoutpity.com) and occasionally pens something poisonous for her personal site, The Redhead Papers (www.redhead-papers.com). She's not fond of doctors, but if her internist looked even remotely like McDreamy, she'd start exhibiting signs of hypochondria and FAST.

The characters—their realism, their quirks and flaws and bad decision-making skills—are the best part of *Grey's Anatomy*. But the trouble with having such realistic characters is that it's hard to find somebody to really admire. Meredith? Love her, but no. So . . . who? Lawrence Watt-Evans takes us through our options.

Lawrence Watt-Evans

FINDING THE HERO

There's a habit most people in our society have of referring to the central character in a story as the hero—it's a shorter, handier word than "protagonist," and after all, usually the protagonist *is* the hero of the story. Buffy Summers was certainly the hero of *Buffy the Vampire Slayer*, Veronica Mars is the hero of *Veronica Mars*, Jack Bauer is the hero of *24*, Captain Kirk was the hero of the original *Star Trek*, and so on.

But "hero" doesn't just mean "protagonist." It doesn't mean "lead character." It doesn't mean "star."

A hero is someone who is *better* than most of us.

The form that takes can be almost anything. But traditionally, a hero is righteous, brave, and persistent—he has the desire to do the right thing, the courage to try to do it, and the fortitude to press on against adversity. To me, that's what makes someone a hero. Strength, cunning, and a dozen other traits are useful, but they aren't what *make* him a hero; to be heroic, you do what's right even when you don't want to, even when you're afraid, and you keep on doing it, without thought of reward.

Well, okay, a hero can *think* about the reward, but that's not why he does it. He does what's right because it's *right*.

Mind you, a hero doesn't have to be heroic *all* the time; he can let little things go. He doesn't have to *intend* to be heroic at all. He doesn't even have to *succeed* at being heroic. But he has to try to do what's right, regardless of the cost to himself. (No risk, no heroism—anyone can do what's right when it's free and easy.)

Meredith Grey is the protagonist of *Grey's Anatomy*—her name's right there in the title, announcing this fact—but if you watch the show for any length of time, it becomes clear that she's not much of a hero. Oh, her heart's generally in the right place; she doesn't really try to hurt anyone, she tries to help when she can, and she does take care of her mother, but a hero? No.

Right from the start, in the very first episode, she fails at the most elementary sort of heroism. She and Cristina made an agreement that if they could jointly come up with the diagnosis for a patient, Cristina would get to scrub in on any surgery that resulted—but when it came down to it, and Dr. Shepherd chose Meredith for the operation, she didn't protest, didn't say that Cristina should go.

Clearly, saying that Cristina should get it was the right thing to do—and Meredith didn't do it.

Eventually she spoke up, but Dr. Shepherd overruled her, and she didn't insist. She accepted his reasoning and broke her promise. In the end, it was Meredith, and not Cristina, who assisted in the OR.

That's just one example; throughout the series, Meredith falls short of what she wants to be, what she *ought* to be. She hides the truth, she lets down her friends, she drinks to excess, she goes to bed with men when she knows she shouldn't. Yes, she also saves lives, she tries to be a loyal friend and do what's right, but all in all, she's clearly not a hero. The protagonist, yes; a hero, no.

So if it's not the title character, not the female lead, *is* there a hero on *Grey's Anatomy*?

Well, it certainly isn't Derek Shepherd, who didn't tell Meredith that he was married until his wife showed up, who favored his playmate over the other interns until Dr. Bailey called him on it, and who generally behaves in a self-centered, inconsiderate fashion when he's not actually practicing medicine. He's a brilliant doctor, sure, we accept that, and if I needed brain surgery I'd be happy to have him do it, but otherwise? He's handsome and winsome—and really, something of a jerk. For the whole second season, he couldn't let either Addison or Meredith go, couldn't commit himself to either one, and wouldn't admit it even to himself.

This is not heroic in any way. And even the surgeries he performs aren't heroic; they're his job, what he's paid to do, what he's trained to do. Heroism is going *beyond* what's expected. There's no risk to him, no cost, in what he does. There's no reason *not* to do it.

So he's not a hero any more than Meredith is. That eliminates the two romantic leads. Who are our other candidates?

At the start of the first episode, after we were introduced to Meredith Grey and her situation, the next scene was a group of interns starting their careers at Seattle Grace. These were the characters we would follow through the series. Do any of *them* qualify as heroes?

The impulsive Izzie Stevens, perhaps? Izzie, who gets obsessed with certain patients, often skirting the bounds of the ethical? Who doesn't have the courage to deal honestly with her hockey-playing ex-boyfriend? Who repeatedly teases her roommate George? Who regularly abuses Meredith's hospitality? I don't think so.

The brilliant but emotionally stunted Cristina Yang? The woman whose biggest failing as a doctor is her inability to see her patients as human beings? The workaholic who's so out of touch with her feelings that she can barely talk to the man who impregnated her, who doesn't tell him she's pregnant, and who doesn't even call him by his first name? No. Heroes can be screwed up, but Cristina is clearly so focused on her career that she has no real concept of right and wrong, and lacks any sort of emotional courage at all.

George O'Malley, the bumbling, soft-spoken, soft-bodied young man who barely made it into the program at Seattle Grace in the first place?

Well . . . maybe, yeah. Let's take a closer look.

When we first met George, he was reminding Meredith that they had met at a mixer, and that she'd been wearing "strappy sandals." He then immediately realized that Real Men Don't Notice Shoes and said, "Now you think I'm gay. Ah, no, I'm not gay, it's just that you were, ah, unforgettable . . ." ("A Hard Day's Night," 1-1).

He had a crush on Meredith, but couldn't even hold Meredith's attention long enough to tell her. First impressions are not his strong point.

In fact, George makes disastrous first impressions. That first day, George didn't impress *anyone*. Dr. Bailey called him a puppy. Dr. Burke chose him for his first surgery because he expected George to be easy to terrorize. When George was about to start that first surgery, other interns placed bets on whether he was going to cry, faint, crap his pants, sweat himself unsterile, screw up the procedure, or simply collapse. They thought he was weak.

But he's not. George didn't do any of those things, at least not initially. He did fine at first, to everyone's surprise. But when he *did* make a mistake, he couldn't recover. Dr. Burke had to take over.

Later in the pilot, though, when he made his second mistake by telling a woman that her husband would be fine, he took responsibility. He was the one who told her that her husband was dead. He didn't hesitate, or run off; he did his best to atone for making a promise he had no right to make and could not keep. He did something wrong, but he didn't try to cover it up; he tried to make it right.

Miserable over his two failures, he told Meredith he should have been a postal worker, because he's dependable rather than brilliant. His family thinks being a surgeon practically makes him a superhero, but he can't see himself that way. He's not a big, strong, handsome surgeon, fearlessly healing patients, the master of every situation. He's just good ol' George.

That hardly sounds like a hero, does it?

But he *is* good ol' George, and he is dependable. You can depend on George to try to do what's right, whether it's easy or not, and not to give up. He's willing to let his perceived betters do the hard stuff, willing to yield to their superior knowledge and experience, but if they don't do what needs doing, he will. He never puts himself forward, but he steps up when he sees the need.

When he was trapped in a broken elevator on the way to the operating room with another, apparently more talented intern, accompanying a heart patient who needed immediate surgery, George stood back while the experts tried to talk Alex through the surgery that would keep the patient alive.

But Alex froze. He was in over his head and he knew it, and he couldn't perform the surgery.

George didn't freeze. He stepped up, did the surgery unaided, without the resources of the OR, and saved the patient's life. When the chips are down and no one else can do what needs to be done, George will at least try.

Later, the very pregnant Dr. Bailey went into labor and refused to allow her baby to be delivered because her husband had been critically injured in a car wreck and wasn't there. Others tried to talk sense to her, but they were all distracted by the series of disasters happening elsewhere in the hospital, all making appeals to simple rationality, and Bailey wasn't having it. Eventually Addison Montgomery-Shepherd, Bailey's obstetrician, gave up on her, everyone gave up on her, but George—George never gave up. It was George who talked her around, who spoke to her on her own terms. It was George who saw to it that the baby was safely delivered.

When anesthesiologist Dr. Taylor showed up for surgery smelling of booze, it was George who questioned his fitness to be there. He chose to do what he thought was right even though it meant opposing those who outranked him.

When Joe the bartender needed surgery but had no way to pay for it, it was George who filled out the grant application to get the surgery classified as research, and who talked Chief of Surgery Webber into signing it.

George does not give up. He sees what needs to be done, and if no one better steps forward, he does it.

He doesn't always succeed. Early on he pulled a shift working trauma codes in the emergency room, expecting to save a dozen lives, but he didn't. Most of his patients died. It was only afterward that Cristina told him that 95 percent of trauma code patients die. He demanded to know why no one told him that before, but you know, watching him, that it wouldn't have made any difference. He did his best, regardless of how many lived or died, because that's who he is.

Nor is it just on big things, or medical matters, where George comes through.

When Joe the bartender collapsed, George, Meredith, and Cristina all rushed to his aid, but when Joe insisted on walking across the street to the hospital under his own power, it was George who walked beside him to steady him.

When Meredith was marching out of the hospital into the rain in a huff, it was George who ran after her with an umbrella.

When Meredith was by her own admission drunk, and headed for her car, it was George who demanded her keys rather than letting her drive.

He's always there doing his part, backing up his friends. When they're doing something wrong, he'll try to talk them out of it, but when he can't—and he pretty much always can't—he'll still do his best to protect them from the consequences.

And he has unexpected depths. When he found himself temporarily sleeping on Dr. Burke's couch, we discovered that he shared Burke's musical tastes (they ended up jamming together) and that he regularly runs several miles every morning, as well. George has a lot going on.

But his friends, Meredith and Izzie and Cristina, don't notice. To them, George is the bumbling nobody they thought they met that first day, and nothing seems able to dislodge that idea.

Olivia, the nurse George dated, doesn't see him as a bumbling fool.

Callie, the resident he hooked up with later, doesn't see him as a bumbling fool, either—in fact, at first she almost idolized him, and when Izzie finally realized this and pointed it out ("He's her McDreamy!" ["The Name of the Game," 2-22]), the others found it hard to believe and rather funny. George? Someone to admire?

I'm reminded of all those people who look at Clark Kent and can't see that he's Superman. George's babyface is as effective a disguise as those unnecessary glasses that Kal-El wears. Callie could see right through it. Olivia, well, maybe she didn't see Superman, but she did notice that Clark's not exactly a loser himself.

Some people *can* learn to see the heroic George. Dr. Burke initially saw him as the weakest intern, but gradually came to respect him and wound up so friendly with him that Cristina was jealous.

Cristina and Izzie in particular, though, never see past the façade. When George and Meredith had their disastrous sexual encounter, Meredith herself said she was the one at fault, and while Cristina and Izzie initially accepted that without question, later they both blamed George for refusing to accept Meredith's apology, even though they didn't know the details. They couldn't really imagine a circumstance in which George was right and Meredith was wrong, despite all that had happened up to that point, all the times that Meredith had been foolish or selfish, all the times George had been brave and generous.

They saw what they expected to see—the mild-mannered intern, not the hero.

And continuing on the subject of how people see George, one of the most interesting cases is how Ellis Grey, Meredith's mother, saw him. In her dementia, she saw him as her ex-husband Thatcher, Meredith's father.

Ellis despised Thatcher Grey. She thought he was weak and worthless, and left him for another man. She therefore saw George as weak and worthless—but when she made demands of him, George still did his best to obey.

Once Ellis had pointed it out, Chief Webber and even Meredith could see the resemblance between George and Thatcher—but they interpreted the resemblence differently than Ellis did. To them, Thatcher was a kind and good man. To Meredith, her father's great failing wasn't that he was worthless, but that he didn't stand up to her mother, didn't fight for his daughter—but when she confronted her father, he said he *did* fight. He merely lost, and moved on.

There's probably more to come on that story, and it doesn't necessarily relate to George in any case, except that we can see that the daughter, while not the domineering workaholic bitch her mother was, is just as incapable of seeing George as the hero he is as her mother was of seeing Thatcher as a loving husband.

Callie and maybe Olivia know better, Burke comes to see George as a fine fellow, and even Alex sometimes admits that George has done something valiant, but most of the characters can't see past the soft features and stammer. They can't see George as a hero, no matter what he does.

Even *George* can't see himself as a hero.

So George is unappreciated, subjected to constant belittlement by Cristina and Izzie—Izzie consistently treats him like a kid brother and refuses to take him seriously as an adult male, while Cristina does her best simply to ignore him. Still, he stands up for his friends, does what he knows is right, and remains true to himself. He's steadfast, loyal, brave, and honest.

He's not perfect; he does make mistakes. But unlike any other character on the show, he owns up to those mistakes and tries to correct them and do better next time. He always tries to do the right thing, and he's always considerate of others.

What more can we ask of a hero?

LAWRENCE WATT-EVANS is the author of some three dozen novels and more than a hundred short stories, mostly in the fields of fantasy, science fiction, and horror. He won the Hugo Award for Short Story in 1988 for "Why I Left Harry's All-Night Hamburgers," served as president of the Horror Writers Association from 1994 to 1996 and treasurer of SFWA from 2003 to 2004, and lives in Maryland. He has one kid in college and one teaching English in China, and shares his home with Chanel, the obligatory writer's cat.

Mothers may not be welcome at Seattle Grace (as Beth Kendrick pointed out a few essays back), but family is—at least the kind you make yourself. "You're my sister, you're my family," Meredith explained to Cristina at the end of "Don't Stand So Close to Me" (3-10). They're definitely family, Melissa Rayworth agrees—but Meredith has the whole "sister" thing all wrong.

Melissa Rayworth

NEXT OF KIN

CREATED FAMILY IN *GREY'S ANATOMY*

G*rey's Anatomy*, which chronicles the delicious misery of romance and all its attendant baggage, could easily be called a love story. From another angle, *Grey's* is a meditation on life and death, reminding us of a bleak reality: that each day might well be our last. Nearly every week, someone—or several someones—dies.

But what if we peel back those layers, ignoring the steamy on-call-room trysts and emergency surgeries and even the epic dreaminess of Dr. Derek Shepherd? Underneath, the show is really about family.

Yup. I said family.

Granted, this isn't the likeliest interpretation. After all, the surgical interns—the five people we care about even when their actions infuriate us—are all somehow estranged from their families. Leading the pack is Meredith Grey, whose mother's Alzheimer's disease makes communication impossible. Not that Ellis Grey was warm and fuzzy to begin with. In the rare moments she recognizes Meredith, her face sours into a mask of disdain. And Meredith barely knows her father, Thatcher Grey, who exited her life decades ago after Ellis cheated on then divorced him. Making matters worse, the half-sisters Meredith accidentally discovered in the second season don't know she exists. Dad never saw fit to mention her to them.

For Izzie Stevens and Alex Karev, childhood was even uglier. Each walked away from a destructive family at an early age, and they're probably better off for having left. Even the interns who speak to their relatives do so in the tensest of tones: We've seen Cristina Yang cringe in the presence of her overbearing mother and George suffer through exchanges with his cartoonish dad and brothers.

Happy families are just as tough to come by within the upper ranks of the hospital. Dr. Webber, who has dodged his wife for decades, discovered in the second season that his lies never fooled her. Several weeks into the third season, we found him living out of a suitcase with divorce on the horizon. And, of course, the one family that has practiced medicine together at Seattle Grace Hospital, Derek and Addison Montgomery-Shepherd, was never an example of solid familial relations even on its best day.

Patients fare no better. Insensitive parents abound, some attempting to block vital surgeries and others lobbying for procedures that shouldn't happen. Often, it's our interns who intervene—risking career damage—because these parents are so freakin' clueless. George did it with the parents of Bex, the hermaphrodite in "Begin the Begin" (2-13), echoing Meredith's interaction with the mom of a girl who'd gotten her stomach stapled in "The Self-Destruct Button" (1-7). Alex spoke up in "The Name of the Game" (2-22), pushing a dying woman to tell her daughter she had cancer. Three examples among many.

But amid all that estrangement and bitterness, *Grey's Anatomy* still manages to depict one of the most loving nuclear families on television: Meredith, Izzie, George, Cristina and, more tangentially, Alex. They're not blood relatives, but this family is as solid—and as traditional in its structure—as any you'll find in the primetime landscape. Series creator Shonda Rhimes says in her blog: "The interns form this odd, dysfunctional family with one another to get them through each day. That's when I think the show is working at its best." I agree, although Rhimes's makeshift family is actually surprisingly functional—and also surprisingly traditional.

Rhimes has created a refreshingly rule-breaking show, offering color-blind casting and a gay character no one bothers pointing out is gay because it's no big thing. But she's filled the show's center with a family structure as traditional as they come. By the second episode, some roles were already evident; others emerged gradually. Meredith reluctantly took the helm as the family's patriarch (yes, patriarch, not matriarch — more on that below) from the moment she allowed Izzie and George into her house. She provided more than shelter, quickly becoming the one they came to for affirmation or to settle their disputes.

They pay rent, but Meredith rules the house. In "The Self-Destruct Button" (1-7), Izzie and George hid in the kitchen to catch a glimpse of the mystery guy Meredith had wall-shaking sex with the previous night. They were stunned to see Derek Shepherd — better known as their boss, "Dr. McDreamy" — slipping out the front door. But rather than confront Meredith immediately, they whined all day before finally mustering the guts to speak up.

Throughout the second season, Meredith's hold on the group remained. Her impact was often subtle, but occasionally she kicked into serious "Dad" mode. In "Something to Talk About" (2-7), when a male patient appeared to be pregnant, Meredith was furious to see his room crowded with gawkers. "What is going on in here? Everybody out!" she barked, shooing nurses and doctors away. Catching sight of Cristina and Izzie among the crowd, she fumed, "You two! This isn't a zoo. You should be ashamed of yourselves." Despite the fact that they had found "pregnant guy" in the first place, Cristina and Izzie scurried obediently out of Meredith's sight.

Hours later, Izzie and Cristina recounted the day's events with George at the bar. "She yelled at you?" marveled bartender Joe. They nodded, looking guilty rather than mad. "We probably deserved it," confessed Izzie. Moments later, they quickly clammed up as Meredith entered and took a seat nearby. They waited for her to make the first move. Realizing they'd been rehashing what happened, she said, "So, you guys really don't have anything else to talk about?" As they muttered a collective chorus of "no," Meredith smiled, forgiving them.

But Meredith uses this power to do more than simply keep the group from transgressing. She also helps them function cohesively. In "Grandma Got Run Over by a Reindeer" (2-12), she motivated them to help Alex study for his board exams, inadvertently setting the stage for reconciliation between Alex and Izzie. Rather than appealing to their emotions, she simply explained that there's a need and she expected them to meet it. And they did.

We saw the same dynamic the following season during "Don't Stand So Close to Me" (3-10), when the interns were rocked by the news that Cristina had been performing Burke's surgeries. As the group pelted Cristina with questions and snide comments, Meredith stepped in: "She made a mistake," Meredith said in Cristina's defense. The interns' anger bubbled up throughout the episode, and Meredith kept warning them off. Her interjections didn't entirely stop them from venting their frustration, but she kept things from escalating. By the episode's end, though, she was a parent who had had enough of the squabbling. Meredith demanded Izzie and Alex let Cristina off the hook and they did. (George didn't, of course, but Cristina's deception put his father's life on the line.)

Our Meredith is plenty feminine, but there's nothing maternal about her. Like Samantha on *Sex and the City*, she drinks like a man and screws like a man (or, at least, like we've always been told men do), lamenting her hangovers without questioning her right to chase pleasure. The character reminds female viewers that the pursuit of happiness, or the pursuit of *anything* for that matter, is as much a woman's domain as a man's. (I know we women are supposed to have internalized that after generations of progress toward equality. But be honest: How many of us practice it on a daily basis?)

114

Even while ministering to others, Meredith is by no means doing what pop culture considers the traditional "mom" thing. She's much more a TV dad. In the final moments of season two's premiere, Cristina joined Meredith at their watering hole, the Emerald City Bar. They were planted on bar stools, barely looking at each other. Meredith was calm, Cristina uncomfortable. Cristina blurted out that she only shared the news of her pregnancy because the abortion clinic wouldn't confirm her appointment unless she designated someone to take her home. She gave Meredith's name.

> CRISTINA: That's why I told you I'm pregnant. You're my person.
> MEREDITH: I am?
> CRISTINA: Yeah. You are. Whatever.
> MEREDITH: Whatever.
> CRISTINA: He dumped me.

Meredith threw one arm around Cristina, resting her head on Cristina's shoulder. She asked no questions, offered no words of solace. After a moment:

> CRISTINA: Do you realize this constitutes hugging?
> MEREDITH: Shut up. I'm your person.

The credits rolled.

Now, the head-on-shoulder thing may be a feminine touch, but there's something classically Ward-Cleaver-with-his-boy-Wally about that scene. She shared a similar moment with George several episodes later in "Let it Be" (2-8). As George struggled with the knowledge that a man saved from a fatal fall by a passing pigeon had been trying to commit suicide, Meredith was the voice of reason.

> MEREDITH: You can't wait for someone to fly under you and save your life. I think you have to save yourself.
> GEORGE (quietly): You mean the pigeons aren't going to come?
> MEREDITH (gently but firmly): The pigeons aren't going to come.

115

It is Izzie, not Meredith, who serves as the family's mother figure. Despite a crushing work schedule, Izzie found time for baking and mothering George (and barging in on him in the bathroom and sending him out on awkward errands like buying tampons) as early as the show's fourth episode, "No Man's Land." Raised in a trailer park by her (presumably single) mom, Izzie freaked when a patient who claimed to be psychic was admitted in "Save Me" (1-8). She explained that she needed to prove he was a fake because years earlier, after Izzie had spent years waitressing to save money for college, her mom blew the money on phone psychics. Izzie left and never went back. But even as she struggled with memories of her undependable mother, Izzie's own maternal urges dominated the episode. In the soft light of the kitchen, she counseled Meredith about the risks inherent in dating McDreamy and fretted over baking the perfect cupcakes.

The best Izzie-as-Mom moments often come when she hits roadblocks. In "Thanks for the Memories" (2-9), she attempted to cook Thanksgiving dinner for the family but was soon overwhelmed. Help arrived in the unlikely form of Preston Burke, who offered a crash course in turkey roasting. But it really wasn't about the food for Izzie; she hungered to gather a family for a traditional holiday moment. The Izzie-as-Mom, Meredith-as-Dad dynamic was visible from the episode's first scene: Meredith dashed off to work on Thanksgiving morning, ignoring Izzie's pleas for help in the kitchen. Unable to stop her, Izzie's voice trailed in Meredith's wake: "I'm serious! You need to be back here for dinner at six, I mean it!"

Weeks later in "Break on Through" (2-15), Izzie let a pregnant teen in on a major revelation: She has a daughter, given up years ago for adoption. "There's more than one way to be a good mother," Izzie told the girl, offering a level of care that veered toward the maternal. It's something we've seen Izzie do with many patients—the undocumented Chinese immigrant in the parking lot ("The First Cut is the Deepest," 1-2) and the ailing quintuplets ("Owner of a Lonely Heart," 2-11) are just a few.

116

But it is with George that we see Izzie at her most maternal. "Alex tries to lay a hand on you, just tell me. I'll take care of it," she assured him in "Raindrops Keep Falling on My Head" (2-1), sounding like a mom counseling her son before taking him to the playground to face the school bully. Since the series began she's been in George's corner, offering relationship advice and a patient ear when he's feeling down. But as mothers often do, she expects loyalty in return. In "Blues for Sister Someone" (2-23), we saw her grilling George about his budding relationship with Dr. Callie Torres. Izzie was every inch a mom with her teenage son, mourning the loss of the easy closeness they once shared and using every tool in her arsenal—humor, charm, guilt—to regain it:

> IZZIE: George, um, by the way, where do you live?
> GEORGE: I'm busy doctoring, Dr. Stevens. No time for chit-chat.

Callie popped in. Within seconds, she and George were giggling and whispering. Izzie couldn't stand it. We knew she didn't want George romantically—it wasn't that kind of jealousy. Someone was taking away her little boy and she couldn't help but interrupt. "Dr. O'Malley, how's all that doctoring going?" she muttered. Callie and George stared with a mix of empathy and pity, like Izzie was the dorky mom who wouldn't go away. Later, she changed tactics:

> IZZIE: So, first you won't tell me where you live and now I am
>   on the outside of your inside jokes with Callie? When did
>   I end up on the outside, George?
> GEORGE: You're not on the outside.
> IZZIE: OK, now you're lying to my face.
> GEORGE: You're being paranoid.

George finally spilled: He was angry that Izzie didn't protect him from getting hurt by Meredith. He decided to return home that night, claiming new ground by bringing Callie. Izzie was in the kitchen alone eating cookies (probably ones she baked) when they arrived. She was shocked to see George and he knew it, but he played it cool.

117

> GEORGE: So we spent the night at Callie's last night, so we
>   figured we'd just spend the night here.
> IZZIE: So . . . you're back, then, just for tonight?
> GEORGE: Well, Callie's here for tonight. I'm, uh . . . it's my
>   room. You know. I pay rent.
> IZZIE: Welcome home.

He nodded. She smiled, grateful.

That scene and many others defined the dynamic between Izzie and George during the show's first two seasons. George, the late-blooming younger child, has slowly found his footing in the world, causing tremors within the family as he has developed. In "Thanks for the Memories" (2-9), as Izzie and Burke wrestled with that turkey in the kitchen, we got the lowdown on George's birth family. He was forced (practically at gunpoint) to celebrate Thanksgiving by hunting turkeys with his roughneck brothers and dad. It was a festival of familial discomfort—*Zoolander* with rifles instead of mining equipment.

Even as they chanted "O'Malley men!" and swept George up in their tide, he remained an outsider. In contrast, frustrated as George sometimes feels in his makeshift family, he's wholly one of them. Izzie drives him crazy but always supports and loves him. His intense need for Meredith's approval may cause him pain, but it has helped him mature.

George's crush on Meredith may seem an awkward thing to reconcile with the family dynamic. But consider that George has always approached Meredith as much with hero-worship and adoration as with romantic love. More than anything, he wants to be seen and valued by her. In "Tell Me Sweet Little Lies" (2-14), George was deeply hurt when Meredith hesitated in deciding whether he or the newly adopted dog should live in the house. It took him nearly the entire episode, but he finally confronted her: "You don't get to choose a dog over me," he said. "I'm George. I sleep down the hall from you. I buy your tampons. I have held your hand every time you've asked. I've earned the right to be seen, respected. To not have you think of me as less than a dog that you got at the pound. So, I'm not moving out. Whether you like it or not I'm staying."

After their brief but disastrous hookup, he was crushed by Meredith's rejection. But his loyalty remained unbroken. In "Damage Case" (2-24), he promised to stick up for Callie in disputes with Izzie and Meredith. But in the next episode ("17 Seconds," 2-25), when Callie complained that George was defending Meredith, he was blunt:

> GEORGE: They're my family. Izzie and Meredith and Cristina, they're my family. I can hate Meredith and I can be angry at her, but I'm always going to defend her.
> CALLIE: So, you don't have to forgive Meredith, but I do?
> GEORGE: If you want a chance to be part of the family, yeah.

In the final moments of the second season finale, when Callie walks in on a post-coital Meredith and Derek, Callie came through for the family. She was shocked to see Meredith searching for her panties and Derek zipping his fly, but she focused on the crisis at hand, telling Meredith, "You have to come now. It's Izzie." As Meredith darted into the hallway, Callie grabbed her by the untied ribbons at the back of her dress, quickly tying them to ensure Meredith looked presentable. Callie's a tough girl. She can handle shocking moments. But this family is a lot to buy on for, especially given that it has two other integral—and very caustic—members.

Cristina is the rebellious older child, one step removed from the group but clearly wanting its support. Her alpha-child needs play out all over this makeshift family: She pursues Meredith's approval while fighting the desire for it, most visibly in "Tell Me Sweet Little Lies" (2-14). We know Cristina usually tells people to stay out of her business, but she allowed Meredith repeatedly to question her decision to lie to Burke about moving in with him. Rather than saying "shut up and stay out of it" (Cristina's standard response to everyone), she let Meredith keep at it all episode. Finally she sought Meredith out:

> CRISTINA: Fine. If you want me to tell Burke I didn't move in, I'll tell him.
> MEREDITH: No. Don't.
> CRISTINA: What?
> MEREDITH: Don't tell him. At least not right now.

And Meredith's decision stood, even though Cristina's relationship was the one at issue.

As Cristina grappled with the subterfuge surrounding Burke's hand tremor, she ran (literally) to Meredith for guidance: Early one morning she burst into Meredith's bedroom, asking breathlessly whether—hypothetically—Meredith would turn in Derek if he'd robbed a bank and Meredith had driven the getaway car ("From a Whisper to a Scream," 3-9). But within minutes she ran off again, determined to handle the situation on her own.

In similar teenage fashion, Cristina bristles at Izzie's maternal behavior. While dressing in the locker room for her first real date with Burke in "Let it Be" (2-8), Cristina compared several dresses. Izzie piped up with encouragement, but got repeatedly shot down:

> IZZIE (looking at the dresses): They're both really nice.
> CRISTINA: I know that. I bought them. But which one's right?
> IZZIE: For what? You're going to look hot in either one.
> CRISTINA (irritated by the compliment): Well, clearly!

In the following episode, the mother-daughter vibe continues when Cristina reluctantly showed up for Thanksgiving dinner with Burke. When Izzie blanched at the sight of him, Cristina reacted like a chastised high-schooler: "What was I supposed to do? Blow off my boyfriend for Thanksgiving?"

Cristina even finds time to compulsively torture little brother George, though he almost seems too easy a target. "Bambi," she snarled in the show's second episode as he chirped enthusiastically about work, "don't say another word until after the hunter shoots your mother." In fact, for all her strength and motorcycle-riding bravado, Cristina remained stuck in adolescence well into the second season. She hated her apartment because her overbearing mother picked out all the furniture. But let's remember that she *allowed* her mom do that. What we allow in our lives says a lot about who we are. In "Deny Deny Deny" (2-4), Cristina's well-coiffed mom was again allowed to call the shots: she painted her daughter's toenails, and only *after* the pedicure did Cristina recoil, muttering, "Give me my toes back."

Her mom had come to Seattle ostensibly to offer support after Cristina's miscarriage. But when Cristina began to sob uncontrollably, mom was no help. Izzie and George tried to calm her, then called Meredith, who promptly hauled Cristina's mother out of the room. "We don't do well with mothers here," she said. "Why don't you leave and come back later." Later, as Cristina lied motionless in bed, Burke entered. He reached out to smooth Cristina's hair, but her mother warned him, "She doesn't want to be touched." Burke knew better. He climbed into her bed, holding her as she cried. Cristina's makeshift family—which Burke seems intent on joining—offered the nurturing her biological mother couldn't.

On the periphery of this classic nuclear family hovers one final member: Alex. He fits awkwardly, not occupying as clear a role as the others. But though he's sometimes reviled and often at odds with the group, his rare demonstrations of true compassion are powerful enough to keep him closely connected to the family since the show began.

Alex rarely opens up about personal things (do we even know where he lives?), but he occasionally mentions his abusive childhood. In "Shake Your Groove Thing" (1-5), he confided in Derek and Izzie that his father's heroin habit made life hell at home. In "Make Me Lose Control" (2-3), he made further reference to that abuse. Alex may be damaged, but he has a strict moral code: Family members can't lie to each other. In "Blues for Sister Someone" (2-23), when a pregnant woman feared telling her husband she wanted her tubes tied, Alex asked several times whether she was being abused. Once she assured him that she needed to lie only because her husband was a staunch Catholic who considered birth control sinful, Alex snapped, "You're husband's not abusing you. You don't get to lie to him and blame it on the Pope."

After the surgery, Alex also couldn't deal with Addison lying that the woman became sterile through "a complication." He freaked on Addison and, later, when the woman's husband peppered him with questions, suggested the guy find a lawyer. His code of honor may be twisted and his harsh honesty may bruise, but family matters to Alex. Even when he betrayed Izzie by sleeping with George's "syph nurse" Olivia, he never lied. Izzie walked in on them mid-clinch, leaving it unclear whether Alex would have 'fessed up afterward.

At the start of season two, upon discovering that George saved Joe the bartender from astronomical hospital bills, Alex hugged George. It was awkward, but authentic. And in season two's finale, Alex put aside his bitterness over Izzie's love for Denny Duquette, gently holding her as she cried over Denny's death.

But where exactly does Alex fit in this family? Meredith managed to describe his peculiar position in "Grandma Got Run Over by a Reindeer" (2-12), which was littered with messy families, from Nadia (whose relatives shattered eardrums when they talked) to Tim (whose scarily happy family caused his head injury by expecting him to hang "Hanumas/Christmakkah" lights) to Dr. Webber and his furious wife, who forced him to attend their niece's school pageant under threat of divorce.

Amid this tumult, Meredith's speech about Alex was priceless:

> MEREDITH (to Izzie): We're not big on holidays. You know that. But we're trying to be supportive because you're having a hard time. But right now Alex is having a harder time.

121

IZZIE: Why does anybody care what kind of time Alex is having?

MEREDITH: Because he's Dirty Uncle Sal! He's Dirty Uncle Sal, the one who embarrasses everyone at family reunions and who can't be left alone with the teenage girls. But you have to invite him to the picnic anyway.

CRISTINA: Um. . . .

GEORGE: I'm still lost.

MEREDITH: I have a mother who doesn't recognize me. As far as family goes, this hospital, you guys, are it. So I know you're pissed at Alex, but maybe you could try to help him anyway. Sort of like in the spirit of this holiday you keep shoving down everybody's throats!

Later in that episode, Meredith spoke of family in her voiceover: "There's an old proverb that says you can't choose your family. You take what the fates hand you." After a brief shot of Cristina and Burke, Meredith and George joined Izzie under the Christmas tree. Meredith continued: "Then there's the school of thought that says the family you're born into is simply a starting point. They feed you and clothe you and take care of you, until you're ready to go out into the world and find your tribe."

That's what this family really is: An "urban tribe," a phrase coined by author Ethan Watters, who wrote a 2003 book of the same name. Like a growing number of young American adults, the interns' work has taken them far from where they were born—both literally and, in George and Izzie's cases, more figuratively. Like so many of us, they spend much more time with friends and co-workers than with their birth families, even sharing holidays and marking life's milestones with pals rather than relatives.

Where previous generations might have begrudgingly accepted ill-fitting roles within their families of origin or endured abuse out of filial piety, the interns have instead formed their own family. It's quintessentially American: striking out on your own and building a world that suits you. But only in recent generations has that American wanderlust extended to building a family from scratch, without benefit of marriage or offspring or legal connection.

Why have urban tribes crystallized in our society now? Faced with the chaos of parental addiction or the loneliness that comes from being rejected (outright or passive-aggressively) for their politics or lifestyle choices, many young Americans have decided that staying true to themselves is more crucial than staying close with those who raised them. With college educations and fairly lucrative jobs, they have the freedom to make such choices.

Watters says urban tribe members often credit their newfound family with making them better people—something that wasn't happening in their families of origin. "The group encourages me to remain true to myself at all times," says a woman Watters refers to as "Andrea in San Diego," one of hundreds of self-described tribe members he interviewed. "With the sense of belonging it gives me, it is easy to take many risks in my life and to stand confidently on my own two feet" (71). She's describing the support that, ideally, families should offer their members. In reality, some families of origin simply don't.

Is it possible that the makeshift TV family first emerged during the early 1970s on shows such as *The Mary Tyler Moore Show* and *M*A*S*H* because at that time the families we saw on television remained idealized in a way most people couldn't relate to? Ray Richmond points out in his book *TV Moms: An Illustrated Guide* that after a healthy dose of family-focused programming in the 1950s (*Ozzie & Harriet*, *Father Knows Best*) and 1960s (*The Andy Griffith Show*), "the early image of TV momhood invariably evolved into the seeming reality denial of the '70s via the likes of the Waltons, the Bradys, and the Partridges. Their motherly heroines all had a way of holding a messier reality at apron-string's length (even if Shirley Partridge never really wore one)" (10).

As television began exploring the possibility of creating families out of friends, the medium may have helped inspire the real urban-tribe families that eventually developed, says psychotherapist Dr. Will Miller (better known as Nick at Nite's "television therapist"). After all, the Gen X-ers now forming these tribes grew up on a steady diet of '70s and '80s television. Miller brings up another motivating factor that's helped inspire urban tribes: Even among happy families, geographic distance is the norm. He says of the Baby Boomers, "We were the first generation to move away, to relocate away. And it was great to get away even if you loved your family. . . . Now, flash forward and my kids grow up and they're a generation removed from an extended family." And yet, he says, this younger generation still has "the critical psychological need for people who feel like family." Miller says Gen X-ers have filled that space with friends and with our strong attachment to on-screen characters, who play a surprisingly powerful role in our lives according to his research.

As families scattered across the country in the 1970s and 1980s, television was pointing out (on shows such as *M*A*S*H* and, later, *Hill Street Blues*) how intensely co-workers bond when surrounded by death and isolated by workload or geography. They introduced us to the concept of workplace as home, yet these shows felt instinctively familiar because they slotted their characters into traditional family roles. When Sgt. Phil Esterhaus said, "Hey, let's be careful out there," to the Hill Street crew, it struck a chord because he was the physical embodiment of the father figure: taller, older, face etched with experience.

Many urban-tribe-centered shows with clearly defined family roles have followed, all depicting groups of various ages whose members hold positions of contrasting authority. And there's almost always a man in charge. Col. Sherman Potter (and Lt. Col. Henry Blake before him) was the boss of the *M*A*S*H* family partly because he was the boss and partly because he was a generation older than everyone else. Same goes for Lou Grant on *The Mary Tyler Moore Show*, a series that bears a strong resemblance to *Grey's*—a single-woman main character carving her own space in the world.

There was a whisper of change in 1995 when, three decades into the Star Trek saga (an urban-tribe-in-space story if there ever was one), Kathryn Janeway took the helm of the starship *Voyager*. But Captain Janeway, very much like Col. Potter and Sgt. Esterhaus, was depicted as a stoically masculine figure, always in control. She never wore leopard-print flats or lost her black lace panties at work, and her raspy voice was deeper than Captain Kirk's. *Grey's* has broken ground by offering us Meredith as patriarch in all her feminine glory. She cries during sex, eats cold pizza for breakfast, and covers pimples with Hello Kitty Band-Aids. And yet, she still leads the pack, guiding them in the best TV-dad tradition. A few female sitcom characters have attempted to combine the patriarch/matriarch role. But Meredith's brand of urban-tribe parenting—and the tribe she leads— remains a rare thing in television drama.

They're all of similar age, holding jobs with identical authority, yet somehow occupying clearly defined family roles. The *Friends* characters were of similar age as well, but they functioned more as a family of siblings than a traditional nuclear family. Perhaps that's because they often appeared to be playing at adulthood, or practicing for it, rather than tackling it the way the *Grey's* characters do. It was as if Mom and Dad were away on an extended vacation and the *Friends* characters were six teens running the house unsupervised. Some characters wielded more power and were more mature than others, but no one truly ruled the roost. The hierarchy was a bit more fluid. Joey, for example, often filled the role of lost little brother. But he was usually too oblivious to notice his junior status, often proceeding as though he was master of his own destiny. We can recognize an urban tribe like the *Friends* crew as a form of family. But somewhere deep down, I wonder if we're hard-wired to respond to the traditional four-person dynamic in a more fundamental way. Our society—and the fictional characters we watch—have proven that the genders occupying each role can vary, and the relationships don't have to be biological or even legal. But we experience a sense of stability when that classic archetype coalesces: A father-figure leads; a mother-figure nurtures; one child seeks independence while the other seeks acceptance.

125

We look to television for shock and for familiarity, and for moments that blend the two. We love situations we'd never experience and people whose lives are more intense than our own. We want to be with Meredith as she drinks tequila at Joe's bar until 2 A.M., then rouses herself when her alarm blares three hours later and she assists her unbelievably sexy boyfriend (whether current or former) in cutting open someone's brain. But we want all that without nursing our own hangovers or worrying that one wrong move at work could kill someone. We also want to see things we know—like family and the familiar dynamics natural to it—to ground ourselves in this world we're watching. So we're drawn to the way the *Grey's* family functions just below the surface in each episode.

Of course, urban tribes don't last forever. Members marry and have kids of their own. New jobs and new priorities take them to distant places. As I write this, only ten episodes of season three have aired, so I can't say what's in store for Meredith and Derek, Cristina and Burke, George and Callie, or even Izzie and Alex. But whether Derek and Meredith have a baby on the way and the Airstream trailer is decorated with their framed wedding pictures by the time you read this, or they're still struggling to manage the overwhelming connection between them, one thing is certain: By waiting until the third season to really make room for Meredith in his life, McDreamy is up against a dynamic that didn't exist when he first hooked up with her that fateful night at Joe's.

She has acquired a family. A real, functioning, protective, we-close-ranks-when-we-need-to family, whose members have pretty strong feelings about this man and whether he's good or bad for their Meredith. If Derek is going to make a life with her, he'll have to make it work with them.

However he manages within this family unit, I'll admit one thing: I don't kid myself into believing that this hopeful vision of family is the *only* reason so many viewers tune in to *Grey's*. I love the romance and the life-and-death drama and Patrick Dempsey's spectacular hair as much as the rest of you. But somewhere beneath all that is another force that draws us to the show: It's our hunger to experience the kind of ideal family unit we'd instinctively love to be a part of, and still have it represent our most progressive, freedom-seeking instincts.

Frequent Associated Press freelancer MELISSA RAYWORTH's feature stories appear in many newspapers, including *The Washington Post* and *Los Angeles Times*. In 2004, she helped launch *Life & Style Weekly*, serving as associate editor before fleeing the world of celebrity journalism. Before that, she spent three years in Beijing as a writer/actress on the TV series *Modern English* and appeared in two miniseries (including a bizarre turn as a young Margaret Thatcher). In 2002, her play *The Welcoming Committee* made the NY Fringe Festival's top ten. She's writing a book about celebrity culture, viewed through the lens of her experiences in China and New York, where she spent the 1990s doing theater and indie films and making blink-and-you-miss-me appearances in soap operas,

Law & Order, and films such as *The Thomas Crown Affair* and *Mickey Blue Eyes*. Melissa lives in New Jersey with her husband and two sons.

REFERENCES

Miller, Dr. Will, telephone interview, Sept. 12, 2006.

Rhimes, Shonda. "The Last Thing I'm Gonna Say For Now. . . ." *Grey Matter*. 23 Oct. 2005. <http://www.greyswriters.com/shonda_rhimes/index.html>

Richmond, Ray, *TV Moms: An Illustrated Guide*. New York: TV Books, L.L.C., 2000.

Watters, Ethan, *Urban Tribes: Are Friends the New Family?* New York: Bloomsbury Publishing, 2003.

A lot of relationships are about learning: learning how to share, learning how to get along (relationships are a little bit like pre-school that way). Burke and Cristina's relationship, though, is more about learning than most—and for Cristina even more than Burke. Cristina, after all, doesn't have a lot of practice at this sort of thing. She's spent her whole life focused on working her way to the top . . . a place Burke already is.

Robert Greenberger

ONLY THE BEST FOR CRISTINA YANG

What does it mean to be the best? You're admired. You set the standard others try to achieve. You get the pick of opportunities. It sounds good—but is it? There's a price to be paid for excellence. Being the best comes at a cost.

To become a doctor requires an extraordinary effort, starting for many in high school and lasting until they become M.D.s. The years in between are filled with long hours, rigorous preparation, and intense competition. Many candidates crack or decide the pressure is not worth it. Those who survive are entrusted with human lives. A handful rise to the top and are considered to be the best at what they do. Along the way, though, sacrifices must be made, and as *Grey's Anatomy* has progressed from season one through the mid-point of season three, the audience has gained a greater understanding of what each of the interns and doctors has given up to get this far.

Cristina Yang and Preston Burke, as intern and head of cardiothoracic surgery, are at opposite ends of the arc from student to highly respected surgeon. And it is through their relationship that we have been able to best understand what each has had to sacrifice, and what those sacrifices have cost them.

When we first met Yang, she was driven, neither warm nor friendly. We recognized immediately that she has stuffed her humanity out of sight, ready to give up family, friends, and loved ones to be the best. At a mixer the night before her residency began, Yang displayed envy toward Meredith's position as the "privileged" daughter of *the* Ellis Grey, but also a single-minded focus on her career. She practically assaulted Burke, fawning over him and his accomplishments, oblivious to the fact that he was speaking intimately to another woman at the time. When he nodded politely and did nothing more, she stammered a bit, flummoxed, and finally faded away, having made an unflattering first impression.

Her unflattering first impressions didn't stop there. She came across to her attending, Miranda Bailey, and even Debbie the head nurse not as brilliant and focused, but pushy, aggressive, rude, and ill-equipped for the human side of surgery—that is, dealing with patients as people with hopes, dreams, and emotions, the very experiences she had denied herself. She aggressively lobbied to participate in every surgery. As she explained: "Surgery is hot. It's the Marines. It's macho. It's hostile. It's hardcore. Geriatrics is for freaks who live with their mothers and never have sex" ("A Hard Day's Night," 1-1). Yang volunteered for risky duties and eschewed tasks she felt were beneath her, despite the constant reminder that she was still at the bottom of the doctors' pecking order.

The doctor who most intrigued her was Burke, not only for his handsome good looks and fashionable attire, but also his brilliance in the operating room; it made him irresistible. During the first season, Yang was quickly drawn to Burke physically. In fact, she was drawn to him with an intensity that she was clearly not accustomed to. To Cristina, Burke *was* what she wanted to *be*: the Best. He was a cool, calm, and brilliant surgeon, as well as extremely attractive.

There was chemistry—no, there was heat—between them, and the passion they displayed seemed to have been bottled up in both of them. And as the seasons unfolded, we learned how each gave up such relationships in order to get where they were when the series began.

What was particularly interesting was how each handled personal interactions, and how they remained opposites everywhere except in the OR, which seemed to make their attraction all the stronger. Just as they were in synch while performing as doctors, they were at first awkward and uncomfortable when they first dealt with one another away from Seattle Grace. Their first real date, dinner out, was a dismal failure until their medical skills were called upon.

When a hospital tryst left Yang pregnant, she kept the information from Burke, intending to have an abortion. Instead, she collapsed from complications caused by the pregnancy being ectopic. Burke was upset that she hadn't told him, but respected her enough to wait until she healed before asking what her plans had been. Then he respected her life enough not to comment on her choice, despite his profound spirituality.

Burke, in fact, exemplified *everything* Yang was not but wanted to be, whether she admitted it or not. The Thanksgiving episode in the second season revealed an entirely new side of Burke. As series creator Shonda Rhimes wrote on the show's blog:

> In writing the episode, I discovered how much of a gentleman Burke really is. Out of kindness, he takes over this potential turkey-making disaster and finds a way to bond with Izzie. Which tells us a couple of things about him: 1) That he can make himself at home anywhere, and 2) That he is in love with Cristina. Because why else would he do what he does on Thanksgiving? He loves her, pure and simple. And no one can tell me otherwise. I do wonder if they'll make it as a couple. Because, I gotta tell you, it killed me to write that Cristina would rather spend the day in the operating room than with Burke. But it was the truth and I had no choice.

Without alcohol to dull the difficulty of socializing, Yang found an excuse to leave and go to the only place she found fulfillment: the hospital.

Yang has often demonstrated her tendency to avoid things that make her uncomfortable. Early on, Bailey assigned Yang to discuss a case with the patient and family. Yang replied, "I'm not a people person. . . . I can't talk to the families of patients. I'm sorry" ("Winning a Battle, Losing the War," 1-3).

As she and Burke progressed from physical fling to a deeper relationship, she was at first appalled by his fastidious approach to himself and his home life. She was then frightened by the cost of moving in with him: her individuality.

When he first suggested the bold step of living together, she tried to fight it.

> CRISTINA: What makes you . . . what makes you think we can live together? You don't know anything about me.
> DR. BURKE: I know you prefer an eleven blade for your LNDs. I know you prefer to say pickups instead of forceps. I know you like your coffee from the cart by the front entrance better than the coffee in the cafeteria. I know you.

Before agreeing, she took him to her apartment and threw open the door, and for the first time, Burke and the viewer saw the real, unvarnished Cristina Yang in her personal pig pen.

> This is where I live. My mother decorated it. I don't do laundry, I buy new underwear. And see, ah, under the table, six months of magazines that I know I'll never read but I won't throw out. I don't wash dishes, vacuum, or put the toilet paper on the holder. I hired a maid once. She ran away crying. Ah, the only things in my fridge are water, vodka, and diet soda, and I don't care. But you do. Still think living together is a good idea? ("Much Too Much," 2-10)

132

Though his answer was yes, and she agreed to move in, she still secretly retained her apartment, unable to part with her individuality or to truly face the intimacy he had invited her into. The relationship hit a rocky point when Burke found out about her lie when the landlord called about a leak. Later in the day he snapped and shouted at her:

> I am Preston Burke! A widely renowned cardiothoracic surgeon. I am a professional and more than that, I am a good and kind person. I am a person that cleans up behind myself! I am a person that cooks well. And you, you are an unbelievable slob. A slovenly, angry intern. I am Preston Burke! And you, you are the most competitive, most guarded, most stubborn, most challenging person I have ever met! And I love you.

What the hell is the matter with you that you won't just let me? ("Yesterday," 2-18)

Burke's profession of love for Cristina was another opportunity for her to confront intimacy and deal with it. She was stunned when he said it and surprised her friends by admitting that she said nothing in return. In fact, she didn't finally utter the words "I love you" until he was asleep and couldn't possibly have heard her.

His love for her continued despite every obstacle she put in its way. Sloppy versus neat is manageable; their core values are where the relationship founders. The Thanksgiving episode began to dig deeper into those worldview differences, and by Christmas, their souls had clashed. When a young boy named Justin struggled with his Christian faith, we learned that it was something that Yang, raised Jewish but officially an atheist, did not share. Burke, in contrast, declared himself a spiritual person and this difference, to him, may be an insurmountable problem. If she can't live with his faith, or accept that he has faith while she refuses the faith she was raised with, then there may be no hope for the relationship.

133

> CRISTINA: Burke, science is the one thing. You know it's the one thing we have in common. I'm an intern and you're not. I'm a slob and you're not. I say I want to keep our relationship private and you go and tell the Chief of Surgery and you asked me to move in with you and now you're religious.
> DR. BURKE: Spiritual. There's a difference.

Episode writer Krista Vernof addressed this fundamental difference on her blog:

> I loved that while Cristina wasn't interested in coming around to Burke's spirituality, she was desperate to save Justin's life. And she was the right person to do it, because ultimately, she and Justin shared a belief-system, so she was the one who could say what he needed to hear. Which is another kind of family, isn't it? It's the "Tribe" thing I referenced in the end—Cristina and Justin are in one another's tribe. Whether or not the same

can be said of Burke and Cristina remains to be seen, because as relationships go, I think Cristina was right—it's easy to differ in terms of cleanliness or age or experience and still have a relationship—but to differ on fundamental philosophical/spiritual beliefs is much, much harder. I'm not saying they can't overcome it, I'm just saying that when Cristina asked "What are we doing? I don't know what we're doing. . . ." that was rooted in a real and valid fear.

Throughout the first two seasons, the wall Cristina had built around herself slowly crumbled, and as she became more vulnerable to the world around her, she became scared by what she found.

At the end of the second season, Burke was shot, and during the surgery to repair the damage, his hand developed a tremor. He clearly needed Cristina for comfort and support, but such intimacy freaked her out. She kept her distance until she had processed the information, and as the season drew to a close, she made a choice: She went to Burke and offered him the succor he craved.

Rhimes commented:

> If you look at where they began at the beginning of Season Two and how far they've come. . . . You just hate Cristina. You hate her when she walks away from Burke after seeing that he now has a hand tremor. And then you see her give that speech to the Chief and you see the struggle. Her struggle to suppress all of her humanity in pursuit of perfection. And in my mind, what we realize is that she is not cold. She is terrified. Scared that if she lets her emotions out, they will overtake her and she will be hurt. And you can't hate her. Because it's so incredibly human and understandable. There's that moment when Burke tells Cristina that he won't bear a grudge and it's so sad because he means it. He doesn't believe she has it in her to stay by his side. And then Denny dies and Cristina watches Izzie grieving and realizes that she has no other option but to go to Burke and cover his hand with her own. Because you can lose someone if you're not careful.

Yang was constantly being confronted with choices and decisions that needed to be made, forcing her to change who she was, who she saw herself as, and she feared losing the edge that had her on the path to becoming the next great surgeon. At first, she walled herself off from forming friendships with her fellow interns, seeing them as competition. What she couldn't avoid, though, were the long hours of togetherness that ultimately brought about comradeship, if not genuine friendship.

At first, she was in awe of Meredith; she was dismissive of Izzie as a dumb blonde ("You are eight feet tall. Your boobs are perfect. Your hair is down to there. If I was you I would just walk around naked all the time. I wouldn't have a job, I wouldn't have any skills, I wouldn't even know how to read. I would just be . . . naked" ["No Man's Land," 1-4]); and she ignored George as a dweeb. Alex she just hated, especially when they first interacted:

> CRISTINA: You're the pig who called Meredith a nurse. I hate you on principle.
> ALEX: And you're the pushy, overbearing kiss ass. I hate you, too.
> CRISTINA: Oh, this should be fun, then. ("The First Cut is the Deepest," 1-2)

George was totally alien to her, a nice guy who just happened to be very good at his work. Still, he wore his emotions on his sleeve, let things weigh him down, and tended to keep the occasional dark cloud over his head way too long. She had no idea how to deal with him. That is, until he hit rock bottom after his miserable one-night stand with Meredith.

Writer Stacey McKee found herself exploring an unusual aspect of Yang as a result of these circumstances:

> Cristina—who prides herself on few things more than the fact that she's not a nice person—suddenly finds herself filling the shoes usually filled by Izzie (or Meredith). Cristina spends her day with "custody" of George—basically, her worst nightmare. . . . She has no tolerance for George's pouting. She doesn't want to listen to him talk about his problems, and yet . . .

what's great about it—is that Cristina still winds up giving George the best possible advice. The advice he really takes to heart: to stop taking crap and demand something more. Which he does. And which ultimately brings him right back to Cristina. . . . Home to sleep on her couch, saddling her (semi-permanently) with custody of George all over again. What comes around, goes around. Karma.

To her shock, Burke and George bonded, becoming friends who did "guy" things together. She wanted to be alone at home with Burke, but she didn't dare interfere with this new relationship without risking her own. She was clueless as to why they got along so well until Burke provided the key.

As writer Elizabeth Klaviter blogged:

> The moment when Burke is most vulnerable is when he is in the on-call room with Cristina. See, I'd always thought (and I think that perhaps Burke did, too) that Cristina loves Burke because of his composure and brilliance as a surgeon. We all know that Cristina looks down on George, who she is fond of, but doesn't respect. And in this moment Burke confesses to Cristina that he *was* George. Things didn't come naturally to him, he practiced. In this moment he sacrifices his poise to let her deeper into his psyche and Cristina, being Cristina, could react in a multitude of ways. While writing the scene, I hoped that she would love him more—and I discovered that she did—and Shonda liked that discovery—but with Cristina you never know. If we the writers don't know, then Burke certainly doesn't know, and I came to realize just how deep his love for her is. Because opening ourselves to the potential of colossal rejection is so very scary and it is the only way true intimacy is built. This is the first time we see them in a truly vulnerable intimate moment and she rises to the occasion.

136

While we recognized immediately what Cristina gave up in order to become the best, it was only much later when we learned what it was that Burke sacrificed on his way to the top. The one time we saw how Burke used to be, like George, was early in the third season, when he fumbled around his exacting mother. Even as he tried to satisfy Cristina's desire not to be alone with the woman, he also tried to mollify the situation by bringing his mother a scone. It's a rare glimpse into what Burke must have been like at the resident stage of his career, putting home behind him and working hard to become a surgeon.

By that point, Burke and Cristina had become a study in contrasts. She stifled her emotional being to concentrate solely on medicine while Burke processed it differently, being cool, calm, and collected as a surgeon but letting himself reap the rewards of the good life away from Seattle Grace. He is a good cook, an outdoorsman, and someone willing to go the extra mile for a friend. But his choice, like Cristina's, to value compartmentalization and control above other, more human concerns, backfired.

Burke has worked hard to achieve the level of "cool" he currently exudes. At the beginning of the series, he was cool, calm, and somewhat aloof. He was perfectly happy ruling the roost—until Dr. Derek Shepherd arrived, and there was suddenly someone as good in the OR (and someone as attractive) as he was, a threat to his position. He was shaken when after all his years at the hospital he was told by Richard Webber, "You do only exactly as much as is necessary. You never take an extra step. You never give an extra minute. You're comfortable and arrogant. And it doesn't impress me. You wanna be Chief? Earn it" ("The First Cut is the Deepest," 1-2).

So Burke, for the first time in a while, was forced to re-examine his life, which may have been why he acted on his physical attraction to Yang. During the course of the first two seasons, Burke had to reinvent himself. It began with Shepherd's arrival, continued with Yang entering his life through the end of season two, when he was shot and potentially crippled.

Burke paid a price for the way he'd chosen to handle his life and career, letting his emotions, once tamped down and under control, get the best of him. Furious that Yang had fallen asleep during sex, Burke refused to let her go and retrieve the heart that might save Denny's life. That set in motion the events that resulted in his getting shot.

As writer Mark Wilding put it:

As for the other thing that might have caught your attention at the end of the episode—namely Preston Burke lying on the ground with a bullet in him—that was a bad thing. At least none of our interns did that. At least, directly. Indirectly's another story. After all, it was Izzie's misbehavior that led to him rushing back to the hospital. Of course, he was being bad at the start of the episode—punishing Cristina for falling asleep during sex by telling her she couldn't go get the heart. Still, it's not like he deserved to get shot.

As season three opened, Cristina found herself in an unusual and not entirely comfortable place: being the supportive friend and loving girlfriend. First, she awkwardly comforted Izzie, locked away in the bathroom, refusing to change out of her prom gown. Then she went to visit Burke, still recovering in the hospital, and told him not to die. Creator Rhimes noted on the blog after the broadcast, "'Don't ever die' is one of my favorite Cristina lines ever. Look at how much she's changed since that night at the mixer." She's changed, but that doesn't mean she's changed her goals.

Upon their first meeting, Burke's mother accused Cristina of being selfish while her Preston was a giver—a volatile combination that she did not approve of. Yes, Yang is selfish but she admitted to being so since that was something she needed in order to be the best. Burke, already the best, is comfortable enough to let his true nature show through. Yang, still on her way to achieving her goals, can't let her shield down, can't display anything that might be perceived as soft. (Except to Burke—hence the striptease in "I Am a Tree" [3-2].)

Yang's fear is that with each crack in her shields, such as comforting Izzie, she will grow more vulnerable, costing her a chance at being the best. She sees, through Burke, that being the best is possible, and so is determined to remain steely until the residency ends.

That striving to be the best also means that when Cristina committed herself to a healing Burke, she was going to be the best girlfriend possible, and the first major character arc for both in season three dealt with the results. Both Burke and Yang benefited from Yang's support: Burke benefited from Cristina pushing him to practice surgery on chickens, and she in turn benefited from assisting him in the OR, edging ahead of her peers in experience. At first it worked well. In fact, Zoanne Clack at the Grey Matter blog noted, "Cristina assures him she'll be there. On his right side. They saved this life together. They pulled it off. They are in love, they'll make this work, but when do you draw the line with love?"

But keeping his tremor a secret did two things—it allowed him to heal . . . and also turned the relationship toxic. Stacy McKee observed:

> Oh, Cristina. Seattle Grace's own Lady Macbeth . . . what can I say about Cristina? She's (barely) holding it all together. She and Burke have started this thing—they have become a team, a well oiled machine, only . . . how long do they really think they can keep something like this up? Theirs is a temporary fix to a potentially very big problem . . . they've barely been able to put their system into place and already, it's beginning to unravel. She is doing precisely what she has to do to protect Burke—whether it earns her points or burns bridges with her friends or her colleagues—she's doing what it takes. Because she's committed.

139

The very walls she erected around herself to get through med school and carried with her to Seattle Grace turned into prison bars as things became more intense. She worked herself into exhaustion to prep in case Burke needed her, and when he did need her, his ego took a beating.

Everything came out in the episode "From a Whisper to a Scream" (3-9). Burke, finally offered Chief of Surgery, beating out Shepherd, was suddenly exposed and lost the trust of his friend and mentor, Webber. Kip Koenig said on the blog, "Burke is a man of such integrity, even if he believes he is recovered—and he absolutely does—not being completely forthright with Derek, or Richard, or Bailey, or anyone, is wrong. He's betrayed all of them and that eats away at who he really is. And so it has to end."

Yang followed her conscience and told the Chief everything, but when she finally got up the guts to walk into the apartment they share, Burke closed the bedroom door on her. Becoming the best, it appeared, had cost Cristina the best.

Still, she was not the same Cristina Yang who charged from case to case at the beginning of her residency. No, even after being shut out by her man, she was ready to stand by him when Burke himself finally admitted he needed help from Shepherd in fixing the hand tremor. At this writing, the third season continues to unfold, and how the relationship will progress remains to be chronicled. It is likely they will continue to need one another's love and support but resent needing anyone but themselves, a complication that will take time to resolve.

Callie Torres pointed out early in season three that on the road to becoming a doctor, each and every person working at Seattle Grace stopped his or her personal development at seventeen. The hospital was high school with scalpels, but now that the residents have settled in and gotten to know one another and actually practice their skills, they're slowly—and somewhat shakily—also finishing the journey to adulthood, the delay just one more price that has to be paid on the way to being the best.

140

ROBERT GREENBERGER is a writer and editor with extensive credits in fiction and non-fiction. Having grown up watching too much television, he feels eminently qualified to contribute to Smart Pop's collections, this being his third offering. By day, he is Managing Editor at *Weekly World News*, where the stories are even more outrageous than anything witnessed at Seattle Grace. He makes his home in Connecticut.

Sometimes, when Lani Diane Rich is in kind of a tight spot, she thinks to herself: What would Jesus (or Buddha, or Gandhi) do? And•when she remembers that most of our spiritual leaders didn't have a lot to say on the subject of feminism or Bratz dolls, she looks elsewhere for guidance. She looks to Miranda Bailey.

Lani Diane Rich

WHAT WOULD BAILEY DO?

A MODERN GIRL'S GUIDE TO BEING A BAILEY

I'm not big on culling feminist icons from TV screens, for the obvious reason: They're fictional. Of *course* Donna Reed could doll up in her pearls and keep a clean house while getting a hot dinner on the table for her husband and kids—it was a fake house and a fake dinner. (I'm withholding judgment on the pearls.) Then there was Donna Reed 2.0, also known as Carol Brady, where the only realistic note was that she had a housekeeper to help her with the six bratty kids. If they'd had her chase the kids around the house with a spatula once or twice, I could have gotten behind Carol. As it was, she was just irritating. And what kind of woman allows her husband and sons to perm? Even in the seventies? For that alone, she should have been taken out to the woodshed and forced to cut a switch.

Gradually, we worked our way up to Claire Huxtable, which ticked me off because she was a professional woman with five kids and a clean house. She had it all, in that classic bring-home-the-bacon-and-fry-it-up-in-a-pan load of crap way they fed us in the eighties. If Claire Huxtable were a real woman, she would have dropped dead before Rudy was so much as a twinkle in Cliff's eye. Not that this stopped any of us from wanting to be Claire Huxtable. Does anyone remember the Cos from back in the *I Spy* days? I'd have become a lawyer for that man, *nooooooo* question. But five kids? Think again.

My point is that television, up to now, has not really provided a real woman your average female viewer could realistically point to and say, "I wanna be like her." The fact is, if we tried to be like That Girl or Mary Tyler Moore or any of the number of women who managed to run a home, a business, and a social life without ever mussing their lipstick, we'd all eventually need to be committed. Which is not a criticism—it's television. It's *supposed* to be fantasy, and as long as the storytelling is up to snuff, it's all good. I'm just saying I wouldn't pattern myself after a television character.

Until, that is, I met Miranda Bailey.

> "Rule number one: Don't bother sucking up. I already hate you.
> That's not gonna change."
> —MIRANDA BAILEY, "A Hard Day's Night" (1-1)

142

Since the moment Miranda Bailey stepped onto the screen, accepted with enthusiasm the nickname of "the Nazi," and made those five whiny interns wish they'd brought a spare pair of drawers on their first day, she has been my hero. It wasn't just her mouthiness, although that was a big part of it—I love a mouthy broad. It was the mouthiness combined with her humor, compassion, and intelligence that made her a character a girl could get behind. As a mother raising two young girls in the age of Britney Spears and Bratz dolls, I can tell you that I'd be damn proud if either one of them turned out like Miranda Bailey. As far as I'm concerned, television character or not, she's my new feminist ideal. She's a professional and a mother, and for the first time in television history, a female character is dealing with that conflict in a somewhat realistic manner, one that is not resolved after a single episode. Bailey gets things right sometimes, and sometimes she screws the pooch but good. And when she does, she doesn't nail herself to a cross in eternal penance for not being perfect all the time. She gets up, dusts herself off, and moves on. Personally, I don't think it's that ridiculous to adopt a *What Would Bailey Do?* model for dealing with life.

At the very least, life would be infinitely more interesting.

TELLING IT LIKE IT IS

"You're interns. Grunts. Nobodies. Bottom of the surgical food chain."
—MIRANDA BAILEY, "A Hard Day's Night" (1-1)

There's this thing women do. Of course, not *all* women, and not *all* the time. But in general, us girls have a tendency to hold our tongue if we think what we've got to say is going to hurt someone's feelings. We want to be forthright and honest, of course, but not necessarily at the cost of people liking us. And that's not a criticism. Take it from one of the mouthiest of broads—telling it like it is is a massive pain in the ass and is very rarely worth the hassle. Also, except for the most sadistic of us, it's just not fun to know that your words hurt someone's feelings.

But there are times, moments, when speaking up is the right thing to do, and on those occasions, telling it like it is is a good thing. Bailey is a master of this, and as far as I can tell, the secret is in applying the proper criteria—measuring the situation up against the Bailey yardstick, which as far as I understand it, goes a little something like this:

They're asking for it. And I mean *literally* asking for it. After a few years of offering my opinions unasked, I started requiring this. Someone would throw out a question and I'd ask them, "Are you sure you want to hear my opinion on this?" Amazingly, more often than not, they'd say yes. If the person's asking for it, feel free to let loose . . . even if it's your boss.

> BURKE: Anything you say in the next thirty seconds is free. Starting now.
> BAILEY: I think you're cocky, arrogant, bossy, and pushy. You also have a God complex. You never think about anybody but your damn self.
> BURKE: But I—
> BAILEY: I still have twenty-two more seconds. I'm not done.
> ("The First Cut is the Deepest," 1-2)

It serves the greater good. Sometimes people are just stupid. They're begging for a verbal smackdown through their actions, not their words.

These are the moments when we want to let loose, when it would be so justified, and it would feel so good. But, no matter how stupid the act, if the person is hurting only themselves, just shut up. Trust me, it's not worth it.

However, if they're putting anyone else in danger? Go for it, tiger.

> BAILEY: Is he okay? No. No, he's not okay at all. He hurled his body down a concrete mountain at full speed for no good reason. . . . You wanna kill yourselves flying down a concrete mountain, go to it. But there are other people walking, people driving, people trying to live their lives on that concrete mountain. ("Winning a Battle, Losing the War," 1-3)

Protecting those who need it. There are times when speaking the truth has nothing to do with you, or the person you're talking to. It's about speaking up for people who are not in a position to speak up for themselves. This is the trickiest of all the criteria, and the one you'll be able to apply only in the rarest of circumstances. And if the circumstances require you to take your boss aside to keep him from hurting his ex-girlfriend . . . well, then you get bonus points.

> BAILEY: She's a human traffic accident and everybody's slowing down to look at the wreckage. She's doing the best she can with what she has left. Look, I know you can't see this because you're in it, but you can't help her now. ("Something to Talk About," 2-7)

Compassion Where Compassion's Due

> "He's someone's husband. Someone's son, not a collection of body parts for you to harvest. A person."
> —Miranda Bailey, "Winning a Battle, Losing the War" (1-3)

The thing that draws people to extremes is how easy those extremes are. It's fairly easy to be super-sensitive all the time, to speak softly and forego the big stick. It's also pretty simple to play it tough and lay down the law at every turn. What's hard, yet necessary, is to find that line in the middle, which is one thing Bailey does very well. In the first few episodes, you think you've got her figured—just another hard-ass beating up on her interns to make a point and take out her aggression. As time goes by, however, we see that Bailey never goes for the hard line when compassion is required. In "Winning a Battle, Losing the War" (1-3), when Cristina wanted to harvest the organs of a man who was injured during an annual, illegal bike race, it was Bailey who explained to her that the patient was a man, a husband, and a father. In "Grandma Got Run Over by a Reindeer" (2-12), when O'Malley made fun of Alex for killing a patient, Bailey set him straight right quick, telling him that eventually every doctor makes a fatal mistake. When Cristina lost her baby ("Make Me Lose Control," 2-3), when Meredith was left broken-hearted by McDreamy ("Something to Talk About," 2-7), when Alex teased a patient with a blushing disorder ("Make Me Lose Control," 2-3), Bailey applied a soft touch to get things back on track. Knowing when compassion is required, as well as when it is not, is a skill worth developing.[1]

THE ABANDONMENT OF PERFECTION

"I sat up one night, middle of the night and I knew I could do this. I still don't know how I'm gonna do this, but, I knew I could do it. You

---

[1] Okay. This may be a good time to discuss the early episodes of season three, when Bailey briefly stopped being Bailey. Her over-identification with Izzie's plight after she cut Denny's LVAD wire, and the needy, weird, and weepy bit with the husband of a plague victim ("Time Has Come Today," 3-1) was not Bailey. You know, I get that she had a baby, and she was insecure with her position in the hospital, worried about being mommy-tracked and whatnot, but still. I didn't buy it. A woman with the confidence and integrity to knock on the window of a car as her boss is getting busy inside and say, "You mind moving this tail wagon? You're blocking me in" ("Shake Your Groove Thing," 1-5), is just not the kind of chick to let mommy hormones completely annihilate her personality. But since the real Miranda Bailey returned somewhere around "Oh, the Guilt" (3-5), when she helped a young mother with breast cancer stop denying her anger toward her child, I've decided to forgive and forget. For the purposes of this essay, because Bailey came back to herself, I'm gonna let the first four episodes of season three slide.

just have to know. And when you don't know, then no one can fault you for it. You do what you can, when you can, while you can. And when you can't, you can't."
—MIRANDA BAILEY, "Begin the Begin" (2-13)

There was a night about five years ago when I had an epiphany. I was up late with a new baby, stressing over something stupid like Cheerios in my carpet or dishes that hadn't been done, and suddenly, the realization hit me.

Who freakin' cares?

That was a great night. See, here's the thing: We, as women (again, not *all* of us, I'm just generalizing in general), strive for a certain level of perfection. The most neurotic, angst-ridden, and exhausted of us are the ones for whom it's still in reach, the ones whose kids haven't yet said a forbidden word during a school play, the ones who haven't forgotten to pay the cable bill for six months in a row, the ones whose homes are typically clean enough to withstand surprise visitors. Those are the women I pity, because they're so tired and tortured.

For the rest of us, there is paradise, because we have been broken. We have stared in the face of perfection and found it to be the source of all evil. We have learned to flip off Martha Stewart and Donna Reed and Claire Huxtable, and it feels *gooooooooooooood*. We made out a priority list and if vacuuming didn't make it, well too damn bad. We answered the door in our pajamas and we didn't apologize when a friend stopped by unexpectedly and tripped over an Easy Bake Oven. We are the few, the precious few, who know that perfection is both unattainable and unnecessary, and so we finally gave up the ghost and said, "Screw it."

This is what Bailey does. She knows she's not perfect. She just doesn't care.

You gotta respect the simple brilliance of it.

BEING A BAILEY

"You're Dr. Bailey. You don't hide from a fight. You don't give up. You strive for greatness. You . . . Dr. Bailey . . . you are a doer. I know your

146

husband is not here and I know there are a lot of things going on here that we have no control over. But this . . . this we can do. Okay?"
—GEORGE O'MALLEY "(As We Know It)," 2-17

It's all well and good to talk about the practical application of being like Bailey, but it's another thing entirely to actually apply it. I think my obsession with Miranda Bailey is due in no small part to the fact that I'm raising two girls. I've heard it said that the strongest role model in a child's life is the same-sex parent, and this has me a little worried on behalf of my darling angels. Not that I'm a terrible person or anything. I do okay, and my chances of going directly to hell without passing Go or collecting $200 are really only fair-to-middlin'. But, like everyone, I've got my faults, and I have a tendency to focus on them with a bit more energy than I expend on any positive qualities I might also possess. So, for example, while I will quickly dismiss the fact that I spent an entire weekend amiably engaging in eighteen thousand repetitions of "Knock, knock, who's there, banana" with my children and laughing *every time*, I will waste days fretting about whether I damaged their little psyches when they overheard my husband ask me, "*Orange* you glad she didn't say banana?" and me reply, "*Fuck*, yes."

(Yeah. Just so's we're clear, when we get to my upcoming rant, I'm well aware of my lack of real estate on any moral high ground.)

Anyway. My point is that positive female role models are currently living in a spotlight in my head. With a strike of defiance stunning in its surgical accuracy, my oldest daughter, who is seven as of this writing, recently asked me to buy her a particular brand of doll. Now, I don't want to get all political about dolls, to each her own, your mileage may vary, *etcetera*, but I have to say, these particular dolls offend me to the very core of my being, and I'm not all that easily offended. I'm not terribly precious about language or sex or violence; my children live in this world, and I don't shelter them from much as long as they're willing to talk to me about it and it's not likely to give them nightmares. I don't mind Barbie, despite her anatomically improbable physical measurements, because Barbie's a grown woman and serves purposes in life other than providing Ken with a peep show. I mean, she's a veterinarian, she's a doctor, she's a princess, she's a fashion model. She's at least got some

147

balance, some interests. Sure, her feet are disfigured beyond recognition, but I think there's a valuable lesson about the true cost of stiletto heels in there somewhere.

But the particular dolls of which I speak? Are children with low-slung jeans and blow-job lips. They don't come with jobs or aspirations aside from seeing how much thong they can show without technically going bare-assed. Every time I see one of these dolls in a store, on television, or God forbid in the hands of a child, a tiny little voice inside me says, "Move to Amish country. There's no hope here."

But then, there in the aisle of the store, staring into the sweet, pleading blue eyes of my oldest child as she grasped for the slut doll, I asked myself for the first time, "What Would Bailey Do?"

Well, Bailey wouldn't care that a perfect parent would not rant in the middle of a department store, because perfection is stupid. So check that.

Bailey would say that the doll was absolutely asking for it. Actually, the dollmakers are asking for it, but let's not split hairs.

Bailey would do what was in the best interests of the child.

So that's what I did.

148

I knelt down before my little darling, took the package from her hands, and said, "Sweetness, I love you. With every fiber of my being, I love you. And as long as every fiber of my being loves you, which will be forever, I will never allow that doll into my house. I will bake you cakes and I will glue macaroni to picture frames and God help me I will traipse around the neighborhood begging for candy with you every Halloween, but if you think for one moment that this particular doll will ever cross the threshold of our home without instantly blowing up in flames due to the sheer power of my disgust, then perhaps we need to get to know each other a little better."

Of course, my daughter didn't accept this speech as the final word, mostly because I was ranting and she's . . . well . . . seven. But that's not what's important. What's important is that, even if she thinks I was being prudish and irrational, she saw me stand up strongly for what I believe in, and someday, maybe, she'll do the same.

And, life being what it is, odds are twenty-to-one it'll be against me. But that's okay.

I can take it.

LANI DIANE RICH is a wife, mother, and novelist living in central New York. You can find out more about her novels at http://www.lanidianerich.com, or find her blogging with her friends at http://www.literarychicks.com. Feel free to e-mail her with comments at lani@lanidianerich.com . . . unless you want to defend the slut dolls. Nothing good will come of that discussion.

Tanya Michaels

WALKING A THIN LINE

THE DICHOTOMY OF HEALING AND
DESTRUCTION AT SEATTLE GRACE

In a television show where all the regular cast members work in the medical profession (and even recurring secondary characters include nurses, a former surgeon, and a veterinarian), a show set around hospitals with Grace and Mercy in their names, you could draw the logical conclusion that the show's central theme is healing. Of course, in the case of *Grey's Anatomy*, you would be wrong.

At the beginning and end of each episode, title character Meredith Grey provides voiceovers that clue viewers in to the theme. Some of the concepts echoed in both the show's main plot and subplots include time, family, anger, gluttony, deception, denial, and competition. However, while there may have only been one episode that *specified* destruction as its theme ("The Self-Destruct Button," 1-7), as far as I can tell, the concept of destruction in its various forms has been the backbone of the series for the entire first two seasons.

Perhaps destruction is an apt core concept for a show set in a hospital—how many car accident victims, broken bones, and gunshot wounds are treated daily in emergency rooms across the country? What stands out for me, though, are the number of cases on *Grey's Anatomy* where the "victim" is also the perpetrator. The most innocuous of these self-inflicted examples are complete accidents, like a teen-pageant hopeful causing herself grave but virtually undetectable injury when she fell doing rhythmic gymnastics ("A Hard Day's Night," 1-1) or the man who inadvertently shot his skull full of nails ("No Man's Land," 1-4). But not all accidents are quite as blameless, as foreshadowed by Miranda Bailey when she mentioned "the stupidity of the human race" ("Thanks for the Memories," 2-9), and evidenced later in the episode by her third-degree burn victim:

BAILEY: Tried to deep fry a turkey. Of course, he got drunk first.

While the memorable patient who was rushed to Seattle Grace with a bomb in his abdomen ("It's the End of the World," 2-16) certainly didn't *mean* to shoot himself with a bazooka, the fact remains that he took unnecessary risks with a hobby that involved live ammo and the amateur construction of weaponry. The guy's never heard of collecting stamps, or considered taking up golf? According to his wife, he even stored the functioning replica weapon in their garage—and they had children. This was a disaster waiting to happen. When he made the brilliant move to go check why the bazooka hadn't discharged, an action more suited to an animated coyote than an educated adult, he risked his kids growing up fatherless, not to mention the many innocent lives his pastime jeopardized at the hospital. He even killed at least one member of the city's bomb squad. Accidental, yes, but preventable. A less grave example can be found within Dr. George O'Malley's family, when his brothers mixed drinking and hunting, then tried to fire a salute in George's honor and shot their dad in the butt ("Thanks for the Memories," 2-9).

Other patients take a more deliberate role in causing or furthering their problems: Kalpana, the woman discovered to have Munchausen's syndrome ("Deny Deny Deny," 2-4); the pain-medication addict whose attempts to argue his way to more drugs resulted in emergency surgery ("Shake Your Groove Thing," 1-5); and the man who kept screwing up his own possibility for surgery because of a thirst-inducing tumor that led him to ignore doctors' orders ("Much Too Much," 2-10). But these examples stemmed from documented medical conditions, more understandable and less disturbing than the "normal" people driven to abnormal acts of endangerment.

The author in "Begin the Begin" (2-13) obstructed his intestines *and* gave himself mercury poisoning by eating his novel in an unpleasantly symbolic attempt to "put it behind him." (I empathize with writing being an occasionally maddening occupation, but seriously? *Eww!* Still, less creepy than the guy who required surgery after eating ten Judy doll heads ["Enough is Enough (No More Tears)," 2-2].) A high school hockey player, in an attempt to delay surgery until after a big game, amputated his own finger with disastrous results ("Band-Aid Covers the Bullet Hole," 2-20). Digby, a man with an "ethos" of pain and deliberate self-mutilation, ultimately got himself killed in "The Self-Destruct Button" (1-7). In another first season episode, "Winning a Battle, Losing the War" (1-3), reckless participants in the no-holds-barred Dead Baby bike race caused multiple injuries, including a brain-dead pedestrian and a biker who left the hospital against Meredith's medical advice only to return with life-threatening complications.

Seattle Grace's ongoing bizarre patient roster is almost enough to give one pause about the city's inhabitants. (On the plus side, Seattle does have lovely ferry boats.) Of course, the destructive behavior mirrored on the show exists all over the world. Dr. McDreamy put it best in "If Tomorrow Never Comes" (1-6):

DEREK: People do things every day they know can kill them.

Some even do things they *hope* will kill them, such as the patient who "fell" five stories ("Let it Be," 2-8) and the troubled adolescent Bex, who bore scars from suicide attempts ("Begin the Begin," 2-13). In every episode, once the main theme has been established different twists on the concept are explored, and the same can be said for the series overall. One variation on patients who injure themselves through deliberate actions was the patient who injured herself by *choosing* not to take action. In "If Tomorrow Never Comes" (1-6), Annie let a tumor on her side grow to such massive proportions that it could not be safely operated on, and she died during surgery. Time and time again, the medical subplots of the show have illustrated different patterns of self-destructive behavior with a range of physical consequences.

But those are just the patients. Wait until you meet the doctors!

Throughout the first two seasons, the doctors' collective acts of destruction and self-sabotage have jeopardized their careers, their emotional well-being, their relationships, their marriages, and even their safety. I love my repeated visits to Seattle Grace, and I love most of the characters (grudgingly, in the cases of Dr. Addison Montgomery-Shepherd and Dr. Alex Karev). Even so, the people depicted on *Grey's Anatomy* remind me of a prodigal sibling, or that college friend so many of us have who we genuinely care about but whose repeated bad choices we can't condone. When this friend asks to meet for drinks, we agree out of nostalgic affection, the hope they've finally pulled it together, or sheer morbid curiosity; too often the evening ends in the other person wallowing in self-manufactured "bad luck" and us biting our tongues, knowing we can't live others' lives for them. That's what watching the well-meaning characters on *Grey's Anatomy* is like—except, instead of restraining myself, I usually give very vocal advice to the television. The doctors rarely listen.

Which may be for the best, since if they all listened to me, the show wouldn't develop as many fascinating complications. To the credit of the writing staff and creator Shonda Rhimes, these complications are almost always an extension of character, not just last-minute contrivances added for shock value. Take Izzie for instance. Dr. Isobel Stevens, in the final episodes of season two, risked her career (and George's, once she called him to come help her) in order to save the life of Denny Duquette, a patient she fell in love with despite never having seen him outside the hospital. Of course, she *endangered* Denny's life first, but that was all part of her "plan" (a desperate, last-minute scheme thought up by a woman clearly going off the deep end). While watching these scenes, my husband and I fired all kinds of rhetorical questions at the television that were summed up pretty nicely by an appalled Dr. Bailey:

> BAILEY: Where was rational thought? Where was cognitive thinking? Where was first do no harm? The morals, the ethical ramifi—where was sanity when you three decided to help that girl? ("Deterioration of the Fight or Flight Response," 2-26)

On the surface, Izzie might have seemed the least likely of the three main female interns to go to such extreme measures, since Cristina and Meredith had established more controversial behavior patterns when they engaged in affairs with attending doctors. Also, given Izzie's trailer-park background and how hard she struggled to put herself through medical school, would she really throw away everything she'd worked for to "steal" a donor heart from the person higher on the waiting list than Denny? It might not be as far-fetched as it first seems. Early in the first season, she was already demonstrating her tendency to get personally involved with patients; she pleaded with a victim who came through the doors brain dead to snap out of his coma, taking his case very emotionally ("Winning a Battle, Losing the War," 1-3). Even in the show's second episode ("The First Cut is the Deepest," 1-2), Izzie broke rules when moved to do so, treating illegal immigrants with medical supplies she smuggled outside the hospital. At different times, both Dr. Bailey and Dr. Addison Montgomery-Shepherd have warned Izzie that she gets too involved, prompting Addison to teach a really cruel "lesson," setting Izzie up to lose a patient and learn more professional detachment, something Chief Webber once did to Addison herself ("Owner of a Lonely Heart," 2-11).

We can safely conclude this lesson backfired in Izzie's case.

And speaking of the Chief . . . it's fitting that the patriarchal figure of the show has such a self-destructive history. Given his leadership position and years of experience, Dr. Richard Webber *should* serve as a role model for interns, residents, and even the attendings. Perhaps, however, he's better seen as a cautionary tale. His past choices led to an adulterous affair with married co-worker Ellis Grey, noted surgeon and Meredith's mother (is that irony or symmetry?), a workload detrimental to his home life, and an excess of drinking. At first, he seemed to have escaped the consequences of his bad choices, still married after all these years and having reached a major milestone in his career. Yet, it was made repeatedly clear that his relationship with wife Adele was tense, and she startled him with the second season revelation that she'd always known about his affair ("Deterioration of the Fight or Flight Response," 2-26). The beginning of season three found him separated from Adele and living in a hotel. And what of his professional life? One could argue that with nurses striking, a doctor living in the basement, the head of neurosurgery punching out visitors on the surgical floor, his neo-natal specialist being sued, a promising intern cutting LVAD wires, and all manner of illicit sex going on in the on-call room and exam rooms, he's lost control of the hospital.

Even with the success implied in being named Chief of Surgery, his impending retirement has been an issue for most of the show. In the past two seasons, Webber has also been a patient of Seattle Grace, once for surgery he tried to deny needing and again when he collapsed due to stress. Friend and AA sponsor Olive Warner expressed her concern that Webber was having an "emotional affair" with the woman responsible for his hitting rock-bottom and that he might be losing his tenuous grip on circumstances and sobriety:

> OLLIE: I still have the right to bust your ass if I see you slip-
> ping.
> WEBBER: I'm not slipping.
> OLLIE: Not yet, but you're making a pretty big mess.
> ("Superstition," 2-21)

Of course, despite the many colorful characters surrounding her, the center of the show is Dr. Meredith Grey, daughter of an absent father and a cold, disapproving mother; consequently, a woman who tries to create a new family from the interns around her. Mostly, I find Mere sympathetic. Being a surgical intern can be a hellish job, as is explained to the audience on a near-weekly basis, and that, coupled with the trauma of her love life and her mother's Alzheimer's, earns her "points for breathing in and out," as George put it ("Tell Me Sweet Little Lies," 2-14). However, in the case of her love life at least, Meredith sort of invited the trauma in . . . after having a few drinks with it and taking it back to her place.

Our introductory glimpse of Meredith was her waking up with a stranger on her first day of an important new job. This was how she geared up for the competitive career her mother told her she couldn't cut—shooters at Joe's bar and getting naked with a guy whose name she barely knew. (The fact that said guy is accurately described as McDreamy is not the point.) Much later, in "Owner of a Lonely Heart"

(2-11), Meredith admitted to Alex that self-destructive behavior was her norm before her mother got sick.

> MEREDITH: I was partying *way* too much, staying out way too late to keep a job. I was the one at the family reunions everyone was embarrassed to talk about.

Apparently, she's under the impression that she's now more responsible; I'm not sure others would agree. Viewers have seen Meredith hit the bottle on several occasions, opening "Enough is Enough (No More Tears)" (2-2) with what Izzie calls "full-on vomit drama" and being too drunk in "Into You Like a Train" (2-6) to help with the initial onslaught of victims. In "Shake Your Groove Thing" (1-5), Meredith spent the night before a vital meeting to determine whether she still had a career "preparing" by drinking straight out the bottle, dancing with Cristina, and getting caught by her resident making out with McDreamy. (Seriously, why would you indulge in a secret affair parked in front of a houseful of about a thousand co-workers?) Throughout the middle of the second season, Meredith's roommates comment repeatedly on how many men she's slept with in an attempt to anesthetize herself against the pain of McDreamy choosing his wife over her. Even Derek Shepherd passed judgment, in bitterly sarcastic terms ("Damage Case," 2-24). Although I totally agreed with Meredith's rebuttal that he had lost the right to call her a whore, I do think she might want to take some kind of oath that includes "first, do no tequila."

157

Dr. Cristina Yang, unquestionably driven and portrayed as one of the smartest interns, also risked her career, or at least reputation, by getting romantically involved with an attending, Dr. Preston Burke. Ironically, this happens *after* she saw—and commented on—the potential side effects of Meredith and McDreamy's affair. For Cristina, the complications included an unwanted pregnancy and an eventual ruptured fallopian tube. Though she and Burke have had a somewhat smoother and more progressive relationship than Meredith and McDreamy (it helped that Burke wasn't secretly married), their love is often rocky and their future is uncertain. And it's not as if Cristina entered into the arrangement blindly, unaware of the problems it could cause (unlike Meredith's defense that she didn't know who McDreamy was during their one-night stand):

> CRISTINA (sarcastically): Sleeping with our bosses was a great idea! ("Make Me Lose Control," 2-3)

Meredith would probably defend their choices, as she defended Izzie in "Deterioration of the Fight or Flight Response" (2-26) when she said that people can't help whom they fall in love with.

I empathize with Meredith not being able to help how she feels about Derek, even knowing he's married. But she could have chosen to stop it before it ever got that far emotionally—in fact, she spent the first part of season one trying half-heartedly to push him away. She said that flirting in their place of work was inappropriate, she accused him of just being in it for the chase, she explained that their being together would be far more damaging to her nascent career than his more established one, and she drew "a line" they weren't supposed to cross . . . seconds before throwing herself at him and making out in the elevator ("The First Cut is the Deepest," 1-2). In a less playful mirroring of this event, Izzie told Denny an entire season and a half later that she "cannot fall for a patient." Which she demonstrated by kissing him ("Superstition," 2-21), leaving me to wonder if we're to interpret *love* as an act of self-destruction.

Sure, love is often thought of as a beautiful thing that can make life more worthwhile. During Bailey's maternity leave, a replacement resident even stated that her philosophy was to "heal with love" ("Break on Through," 2-15). Yet time and again, viewers are shown the perils of love.

How did falling for Ellis Grey improve Richard Webber's life? Falling in love—and sleeping with—Addison Montgomery-Shepherd cost Mark Sloan his best friend and netted him lots of pain when Addie eventually followed her husband to Seattle.

> MARK: My $400-an-hour shrink says . . . I'm self-destructive and self-loathing to an almost pathological degree.
> MEREDITH: We do have a lot in common. ("Yesterday," 2-18)

She wasn't wrong. The unofficial motto of the show could be "Bring on the McPain." While Mark was missing Addie back in Manhattan, Addison had uprooted her life to win back a husband who was clearly and publicly in love with someone else.

In "Blues for Sister Someone" (2-23), violinist Eugene Foote loved his music so much that he decided to have the pacemaker that was destroying his rhythm and art removed, a decision he paid for with his life. Bailey risked pregnancy complications when her determination not to lose ground in the career she loved caused pre-term labor ("Tell Me Sweet Little Lies," 2-14). Mother of quintuplets Dory Russell made the decision, out of love, to keep all five babies, then later tragically second-guessed herself when she saw the number of health problems the babies had and one infant died anyway ("Much Too Much" and "Owner of a Lonely Heart," 2-10 and 2-11). A surgical intern from Mercy West who stayed long hours for a job *he* loved, nobly helping to save a life, then fell asleep behind the wheel, plowed into another family, and killed a young pregnant woman ("Damage Case," 2-24). Nice guy George O'Malley let his love for Meredith convince him go to bed with her, which resulted in probably the worst sexual encounter of his life, humiliation, and temporary homelessness—but on the upside, at least she didn't give him syphilis.

159

If Bailey often serves as the conscience of Seattle Grace, then Cristina serves as cold logic in the face of sentiment. When an inmate who swallowed razor-blades to get out of solitary confinement explained that she ended up in prison after a burglary gone wrong, something she did to keep her boyfriend from leaving her, Cristina was unmoved ("Owner of a Lonely Heart," 2-11). She was similarly exasperated by Mrs. Siebert, a patient trying to explain why she stayed with an abusive husband, in "Enough is Enough (No More Tears)" (2-2):

MRS. SIEBERT: Have you ever been in love, doctor? Have you?
CRISTINA: Love has its limits.

Yet even Cristina can't avoid the emotion or the havoc it wreaks. During Chief Webber's individual interrogations in "Losing My

Religion" (2-27) to find out exactly what happened with Denny Duquette, Cristina experienced an uncharacteristic breakdown, tearfully lamenting her loss of the edge she desperately wanted back. When we first met Cristina in season one, she was a competitive, hug-phobic loner who rode a motorcycle, avoided her family, and was not looking to make friends. Yet as the show progressed, she's gone from naming Meredith as her "person" on medical documents ("Raindrops Keep Falling on My Head," 2-1) to entering a real relationship with Preston Burke and giving up her apartment—her slovenly sanctuary and possibly the biggest symbol of her independence—to move in with him.

Becoming more emotionally involved with people, however, meant more emotional vulnerabilities, which was demonstrated poignantly and painfully when Cristina froze during Burke's operation, panicking and losing all the clinical focus she'd been taught as a surgeon ("Deterioration of the Fight or Flight Response," 2-26). During the next episode's scene with the Chief, she realized how much she'd changed, letting Burke and the other interns into her life.

160

> CRISTINA: I can't tell you what happened in that room. I can't tell you, and, before, I could have. No guilt, no loyalties, no problem. Before. Before, I wouldn't have even been in that room. I wouldn't have gotten involved. ("Losing My Religion," 2-27)

She turned the tables on the Chief, interrogating *him*, asking how she could go back to who she once was. Webber dismissed her from questioning, saying he wouldn't want to give her any answers that would make her less human.

So that's the other side of the coin, then? That the love we experience, which can lead to devastating pain and cause us to do dumb-ass things, also makes us people? Sometimes better people? How often does callous Alex melt your heart when he lets himself be swayed by affection for others and lowers his guard, be it for a girl in a wheelchair ("Something to Talk About," 2-7) or Izzie? When Denny died, I didn't cry until Alex, who didn't like the guy to begin with and was disgusted with Izzie's actions, pulled her away from Denny's deathbed and cradled her

("Losing My Religion," 2-27). I suppose love, like the show itself, waffles between disturbing examples of destruction—people yelling at each other in the stairwell, on the emotional side of things, and strangers impaled together, on the physical—and demonstrations of healing and making people whole again.

As Meredith pointed out in "Make Me Lose Control" (2-3), the upside of falling is that it gives your loved ones the opportunity to catch you. In life, maybe we need the stupid mistakes to learn from and the moments of tragedy that ultimately bring us together, as well as the more pleasant shared joys and the power of love that help us transcend our own flaws and selfishness. At any rate, the dichotomy makes for damn good television.

Award-winning author TANYA MICHAELS doesn't think of herself as self-destructive, although she does experience both weakness and addiction when it comes to shows such as *Grey's Anatomy*, *Veronica Mars*, *Battlestar Galactica*, and *Project Runway*. When she's not glued to the television, she writes funny, heartwarming romance novels and, under the name Tanya Michna, more serious women's fiction.

Grey's Anatomy is a show full of technically inappropriate relationships that we can't help rooting for. It's populated with people we love—except when they choose their wife over their girlfriend—and people we hate—except when they cradle their friend in their lap while she cries in her dead fiancé's hospital room. Clearly, it's a show full of gray areas, of questionable romantic decisions and even more questionable moral choices. But all that, Evelyn Vaughn says, is just the beginning.

Evelyn Vaughn

SHADES OF GREY

AMBIGUITY IN *GREY'S ANATOMY*

Admit it: The difference between good shows and lousy shows is hard to miss. You've got *My So-Called Life*, and then you've got *Saved by the Bell: The New Class*. You've got *Buffy the Vampire Slayer*, and then you've got *Emily's Reasons Why Not*. While even the worst shows to get aired are probably better (if marginally) than the stuff most of us could film in our basements—in production values if nothing else—few of us need struggle to separate the wheat from the chaff. But what about when it's all wheat?

It's when we start analyzing the difference between the various really good shows that the line gets blurry. *House* vs. *Chicago Hope*. *Veronica Mars* vs. *Freaks and Geeks*. And we insist on doing that, with Emmy awards and Golden Globes and viewer polls, as if a drama's quality could be measured as simply as we measure height or speed or weight. So fine. Let's try it.

Here, for what it's worth, is one measuring stick to consider. Good shows should do almost everything (casting, acting, music, writing) very, very well.

Great shows do that, and more.

I didn't initially watch *Grey's Anatomy*, when it started in the spring of 2005. My bad. I came into it during the second season, just in time for the two-parter "It's the End of the World" and "(As We Know It)" (2-16 and 2-17)—you know, the Christina Ricci, Kyle Chandler, baby-and-bomb episode? By the time I'd reached the end of the second season, and rushed out to watch the first season on DVD, I knew I was in the presence of TV greatness.

But *why*, exactly?

Sure, the cast of *Grey's Anatomy* is outstanding: talented, diverse, and deeply (not just superfluously) attractive. The writing is incredible, thanks in no small part to series creator Shonda Rhimes. But see . . . I could praise all that about several shows.

The music rocks (thank goodness, since the series is set in Seattle)— I bought the CD soundtrack without a single scene of characters going to a club or dance and screaming, "Hey, look, it's Tegan and Sara!" à la *The O.C.* Or *Smallville.* Or *Charmed.* But that's not enough to make the difference, either.

Finally, after multiple enthusiastic viewings, it occurred to me. The greatness of *Grey's Anatomy* isn't just that it excels in its plots, characters, setting. It would need to do all that just to be really good. What makes it great is what it does differently, better than any other show I can think of.

Ambiguity.

No, I wouldn't have immediately listed "ambiguity" on my list of greatness criteria either—that's why I'm so blown away to recognize what a punch so subtle a quality carries.

Grey's Anatomy is great because, among other fine qualities, it doesn't let us rest on a simplistic, either/or view of life.

EITHER/OR?

I don't much like either/or thinking—what logic textbooks call the fallacy of "false dichotomy"—but even I fall into it sometimes. As with most things, either/or thinking is most frightening in its extremes: A radio talk-show host screaming, "Are you a Christian, or are you an atheist?" (despite that Jews, Hindus, Buddhists, Moslems, pagans, even agnostics, by definition, are not atheists, either). Teenagers saying, "Either you're with us, or you're against us," in an attempt to shame another teen into some major mistake just to prove he's "with" them. A politician declaring that anyone who does not support this particular war/proposition/amendment must by definition be unpatriotic.

At its worst, either/or thinking—presenting two options as if nothing else exists between—attempts to manipulate slower thinkers into ignoring the many other, possibly better, options before them. It denies answers like, "I'm a Unitarian-Universalist," or "I'm your friend, which is why I won't help you steal that car," or "Hello—this country was founded on rebellion and debate, so let's tone down the rhetoric and explore all our options."

Luckily, we rarely see the scarier extremes of either/or thinking on our dramatic television series . . . even the Democratic *West Wing* brought in the clever Republican character of Ainsley Hayes to argue the other side. Comedy, like the old *Murphy Brown* series or *South Park*, sure. Some cable channels, like FOX News . . . yeah. But the dramas have to be at least a little more subtle if they're going to win over viewers for very long.

This isn't to say they don't lean in certain directions, politically or morally. In fact, for the purpose of this essay, I'm saying that many of the otherwise great shows *do* show bias, and why wouldn't they? As Abraham Lincoln said, you can't please all the people all the time. No, I'm saying that they aren't as blatant about it as an extremist radio talk-show host or desperate teenagers.

165

But even at its best? Either/or thinking is lazy and misleading. By simplifying the world into sets of two—black and white, with no overlap—it ignores a wealth of reality in between.

Consider *Law & Order* and its gender struggles. You may remember that in its earliest incarnation, the show was all about the guys—not just men but, considering that they were macho cops, *Men*, with a capital M. Several seasons in, responding to criticism about this, popular male characters were replaced in order to bring in a female lieutenant (Lt. Anita Van Buren, replacing Capt. Donald Cragen) and a female assistant district attorney (Claire Kincade, replacing ADA Paul Robinette). While the handling was arguably clumsy—a female character could have been written in without axing other popular figures right away—the idea behind the change seemed valid enough. Except . . . the female characters were still defined somehow by their femininity. They were more than just women; they were Women. Lt. Van Buren is a mother with children and, perhaps more significant, she earned the scorn of her supervisors by arguing that she'd been passed by for a promotion because she was female. This wasn't shown with a great deal of sympathy. Claire Kincade ended up having an affair with Executive ADA Jack McCoy, the ADA after her was a single mother, and another one turned out to be a lesbian. In fact, the ADA—an assistant role—has been played as a Woman ever since, about five of them so far. The one female character the show had from the start, nurturing psychologist Elizabeth Olivet, was raped in one episode by her dentist. In other words, with the possible exception of DA Nora Lewin, there were rarely lead characters on *Law & Order* who just happened to be women. In contrast to the show's standard of manly Men, they have been Women with a capital W. Black and white. Either/or, with extremes as the two choices.

I don't mean this as criticism of a show I really do enjoy. If it were not already a truly good show, we could dismiss the dichotomy as simple clumsiness—but no, this either/or subtext slipped into an otherwise solid work. The creators did somewhat better in casting the leads of their *Special Victims Unit* incarnation (hooray for Det. Olivia Benson) and even better—at blurring the lines, I mean—with Det. Alex Eames for *Law & Order: Criminal Intent*. I have yet to examine how the original show handles the introduction of its first female detective lead in the fall of 2006, but I'm hopeful.

Still, talking about a lack of overlaps, consider *ER* and its racial diversity. Again, this is an excellent show, especially in its hey-day, and its efforts at a racially diverse cast are appreciated. And yet . . . did you ever notice that, more often than not, the race of the non-Caucasian protagonists is very often used as an Issue, sometimes for a Very Special Episode? Even the character of "Deb" Chen, who first appeared in 1995 as a brilliant and driven rival to John Carter, returned in 2000 declaring that she had reverted to using her "real" name of "Jing-Mei" Chen. Just in case, you know, we didn't notice before that she was Chinese. While I enjoy characters who embrace their own ethnicity, this wouldn't have felt anywhere near as forced if they hadn't, well . . . pushed it so hard. As it was, the reversion of Jing-Mei's name felt like forced political correctness. As if a person is either a Caucasion, or a Person of Color, without a whole spectrum of possibilities in between.

166

Maybe part of my problem is that I'm something of a consistency Nazi. I had trouble embracing Willow's fourth season lesbianism on *Buffy the Vampire Slayer*, after we'd had three seasons of her being in love with Xander and Oz. Her lover, Tara? No problem. Heck, I had trouble with Ellen Morgan's realization of her lesbianism on *Ellen*, simply because it came four seasons into a series that, until then, had shown Ellen dating men and in love with her former roommate Adam Green. It didn't matter to me that Ellen DeGeneres herself was a lesbian . . . the actor is not the character. But the seeming retroactive continuity, as with Willow, also felt either/or—as if a person is either straight or gay, and no true bisexuals exist in the world of network television . . . except perhaps in the mind-bending arena of *Nip/Tuck*, which is a whole 'nother essay!

Have I ticked anyone off yet? Sorry. Please understand that I'm naming what I consider excellent shows (especially *Buffy*). And I think *Grey's Anatomy* particularly excels when measured against the *already great*.

Being well-written, all the shows I've provided as examples also have instances of beautifully explored gender spectrums, sexuality spectrums, moral spectrums. But what I've recognized is that you have to search *Grey's Anatomy* not for those exceptions, but for the simplistic extremes. Far more often, it rejects either/or, right-and-wrong thinking:

167

> IZZIE: What if you were me?
> CRISTINA: Well I wouldn't have fallen in love with a patient.
> IZZIE: You fell in love with an attending.
> CRISTINA: Well, so did Mere, what's the point?
> MEREDITH: The point is we can't help who we fall in love with.
> GEORGE: Shyeah. ("Deterioration of the Fight or Flight Response," 2-26)

That's what I'm enjoying—the exploration of the in between. The overlap. One of my favorite symbols, the *vesica piscis* (or chalice-well design), shows two circles overlapping to create a third, fish-like symbol between them. The exciting part is that almond-shaped overlap, the subset between past and future that creates the now, the gray area where right and wrong mingle to make . . . something else, something less simplistic, something more realistic. And more than perhaps any other primetime show, *Grey's Anatomy* is all about refusing extremes for the in between.

GENERALIZED AMBIGUITY

Let's start with the broad stuff, the easy stuff to spot, like the incredible diversity of the characters on *Grey's Anatomy*. True, a slight majority of our leads—like Meredith, George, Izzie, Alex, Derek, and Addison—are still the standard Caucasians that, for better or worse, we've come to expect from a network TV ensemble cast. But the show has far more than token characters of color, as well. Chief Webber, and Doctors Bailey and Burke, aren't just black—they're authority figures. Cristina Yang and the second season addition of Callie Torres keep Seattle Grace looking far more representative of our true population than, say, *House* or the old *Chicago Hope*. I love *House*. But really—one black guy in the entire cast? As mentioned earlier, *ER* does pretty well with diversity, too (how many shows give us characters of Indian descent, as in from India? I can name about three, total, four with the arrival of *Heroes*). But something I've loved about *Grey's Anatomy* is that, thus far at least, nobody's race has been capitalized on for a Very Special Episode. We aren't seeing their races as the extreme end of a spectrum; it's just who they are. Oh, there's the occasional grin when a visiting doctor doesn't realize Bailey could possibly be the person referred to as "the Nazi," but that's as likely a false assumption about her gender as her race. For the most part, the characters are people who just *happen to be* white, black, Asian, or Latino—they can be proud of and representative of their race without making a cause out of it—and there lies a touch not just of diversity but *ambiguity*, of in between. As Cristina put it when Izzie asked her to translate for a Chinese patient: "I grew up in Beverly Hills. The only Chinese I know is from a Mr. Chow's menu. Besides, I'm Korean" ("The First Cut is the Deepest," 1-2).

Even more refreshing? Cristina said this and dismissed the matter, without dwelling on any assumed insult on Izzie's part.

The mix of genders in the show, unlike my aforementioned early *Law & Order* example, is equally . . . well . . . equal. Almost exactly equal, if you do the count. But is there ambiguity, or have we mainly got manly Men and womanly Women?

Are you grinning yet? Contrast the characters of Cristina and George. Which one has a more stereotypically guy-like attitude, and which has a more stereotypically feminine attitude? Hint: Men are supposedly more competitive, and women are supposedly more sensitive. Or how about the wonder that is Dr. Miranda Bailey? She comes across about as girly as a drill sergeant. She's not particularly masculine, despite her confidence and aggression. She's not especially feminine, despite the episode in which she gave birth and her later concerns about being "Mommy-tracked." Bailey is simply—Bailey. These are the more obvious examples of gender overlap within the show. But if you look at the patients, you see even more explicit efforts at showing ambiguity.

Consider the character of Bex Singleton, in the episode titled "Begin the Begin" (2-13). Bex was a teenage girl who preferred her nickname to the given name of "Rebecca" and who presented with an enlarged pelvic lymph node. Her blood tests revealed that she'd been taking birth control pills, and she confessed her reason to George: "I'm as flat as a board. . . . Boobs, dude." It turned out she wanted to "be normal for once in [her] life." Alas for Bex, "normalcy"—however that may be defined—proved tricky. The biopsy revealed a testis. Bex was a hermaphrodite, news that her parents didn't take well.

169

> MRS. SINGLETON: She's, she's a girl. She looks like a girl; she has always been a girl.
> GEORGE: It at least helps explain why she feels so different.
> PSYCHIATRIST: The point is that biologically and emotionally speaking, she has a choice to make.
> MRS. SINGLETON: A choice?

They did not want to give Bex that choice. In fact, they asked Addison to remove any "boy parts" Bex might have while removing the benign tumor—without ever telling Bex the truth. Only because George refused to lie to her did Bex learn what was going on. Bex's reaction? "Oh my God. Does this mean . . . does this mean I could be a boy?" And then Bex whispered, "Yes."

When George checked in on his patient later in the episode, the following exchange took place:

> BEX: George, do I have to be a boy now?
> GEORGE: No. No.
> BEX: But I can if I want to.
> GEORGE: Yeah you can, if you want.

The avoidance of either/or couldn't possibly be clearer. Instead of being forced into a preset definition, Bex could choose gender or choose to exist in between. At that point Bex asked George for a pair of scissors, for a haircut—a task that Bex's mother graciously took over, halfway through.

The story of Bex is hardly the only example of gender ambiguity in *Grey's Anatomy*. In the season one finale, "Who's Zoomin' Who?" (1-9), Burke's friend Bill turned out to have an ovary and was apparently sterile—raising significant questions about how his wife managed to get pregnant. Or, speaking of pregnancy, the episode "Something to Talk About" (2-7) presented us with Shane Herman, a man whose apparent pregnancy—he even tested positive with a home test—seemed even more advanced than his wife's. True, it turned out that he wasn't pregnant. He had a "mesenteric teratoma," a clump of cells he'd had all his life but which had recently began to grow a jaw, teeth, hair. And yet, Shane asked Meredith not to let the teratoma be passed around as an object of display—almost protective of it, as a parent might be of a deformed child. That's three clear examples in which there's male, there's female, and there's quite a lot of gray in between.

If you continue to explore the weekly patients, and the choices they must make, you'll see numerous other blurred lines avoiding right-or-wrong simplicity even when an either/or choice must be made. There's the violinist who wanted a dangerous surgery to remove his needed pacemaker, because the rhythm of it destroyed his ability to play as well as he once could—both sides of the argument, to live without his music or to risk death to keep it, can be credibly made. Two sweet-natured strangers were impaled during a train wreck, and the doctors had to choose which one to kill in order to save the other—a clear either/or decision in which the fact that there was no middle choice was a tragedy.

A man arrived in the hospital with nails in his head and had the choice of five-to-ten "good years" after an extreme surgery that could cost him his memory and personality, or only three-to-five years with his memory intact. In each case, a choice had to be made, *was* made. But in each, that choice was by no means easy or clear-cut.

But wait! There's also the. . . .

MORAL AMBIGUITY

Quick! How many television shows can you name in which the protagonists—the good guys—are adulterers?

That's what I thought. Not a whole hell of a lot. And yet it's not just Chief Webber and Meredith's mother Ellis Grey who had an affair, itself not simple—as Meredith put it to Webber, in "Losing My Religion" (2-27), "It was you. You were the reason my parents broke up. And it wasn't just an affair. She really loved you. She left her husband for you, but you stayed with your wife . . . because it was the right thing to do."

No, the *central pairing* in *Grey's Anatomy* started as an adulterous romance, even though the adulterous aspect didn't become clear until the end of the first season. I'm talking Meredith—the Grey of the title—and Dr. Derek Shepherd, a.k.a. McDreamy.

Sure, their initial adultery can be qualified six ways to Sunday. They were drunk when they first met. Meredith didn't realize Derek was married until his wife, Dr. Addison Montgomery-Shepherd, appeared at Seattle Grace. And Derek was separated from his wife at the time, for his own good reasons. Addison herself explained it best in the first episode of season two, "Raindrops Keep Falling on My Head," after a pregnant patient asked to have Meredith removed from her case for being a husband-stealing bitch:

> Since I lack Dr. Grey's class and patience, I'm going to set the record straight. My husband didn't cheat on me. I cheated on him. So the wronged woman here? Dr. Grey. I think you owe her one hell of an apology.

171

Which, beyond the whole "they were drunk," "he was wronged," and "Mere didn't know" qualifications, is what has made the triangle of Meredith, Derek, and Addison so exceptional, and so beautifully ambiguous. Addison could easily have been played as the villain in this story. But from the start, it's clear that she, too, is no worse than a flawed human being. Yes, she wants her husband back. But this doesn't mean she doesn't understand Meredith's pain and do everything she can to befriend the intern. In fact, all three of the characters feel badly about the role they've played in the situation. In "Raindrops," Meredith mused:

> I wore my new lip gloss because my ex-boyfriend's wife looks
> like Isabella freakin' Rossellini and I'm like . . . me. I'm trying
> to outdo her when she's the victim here, how crazy is that? . . .
> I am an evil mistress.

In "What Have I Done to Deserve This?" (2-19), Addison's guilt over her previous infidelity with Derek's friend Mark ("McSteamy") — who recently appeared at the hospital to open old wounds — colored her acceptance of her horrible case of poison oak in a, well, private area. When Bailey asked how it happened, Addison answered, "I slept with Mark!"

> BAILEY: Oh! . . . And he had poison oak on his—
> ADDISON: No! I slept with Mark a year ago and apparently
>   this is what I get!
> BAILEY: Yeah. But how did you—
> ADDISON: I live in a trailer. I have Meredith Grey's dog. And
>   I went outside to throw a stick and I had to pee. So I squat-
>   ted! Because I didn't want to go inside and wake up my
>   husband because of the way he's been looking at me since
>   yesterday. I just wanted a few minutes of peace. And this is
>   what I get.

As she asked her husband, after revealing her embarrassing condition to him: "So are we even yet? I mean is this bad enough? Have we repaid my debt to society?"

172

In so many shows, we would see the wife and lover characters as polar opposites: one sympathetic, the other not. Not on *Grey's Anatomy*.

Even Derek, who generally acts like the wounded party of the trio, finally saw some of his own responsibility in the earlier deterioration of his marriage in the episode "Band-Aid Covers the Bullet Hole" (2-20):

> DEREK: I was indifferent. You know, in New York. Before Mark. I was just . . . indifferent towards you.
> ADDISON: Yes.
> DEREK: I was absent.
> ADDISON: Yes.
> DEREK: I'm partly to blame for what's happened to our marriage.
> ADDISON: Yeah.
> DEREK: I'm sorry. . . . I'm working on it.

None of which might make true adultery okay, but it certainly makes it difficult to vilify any of the three characters caught in this particular example. In fact, it's the tension between the choices, as *Grey's* refuses to resolve it, that becomes the most interesting part. That's the power of ambiguity. Things can go either way.

Or how about the professional/moral issue of romantic pairings between surgeons and interns? Relationships in which one figure is more powerful—between boss and subordinate, between teacher and student or, oh, between doctor and patient—usually make me pretty uncomfortable. But not, somehow, on *Grey's Anatomy*. All the qualifications that make the Derek/Meredith romance palatable, despite the adultery, also work as a balm for the fact that he is her boss's boss. Similarly, with Burke and Cristina, the two characters are so matter-of-fact about their relations that it somehow seems less . . . wrong.

> MEREDITH: After all this time, all your warnings about me sleeping with my boss and you're doing the same exact thing.
> CRISTINA: Oh, it's not the same thing.
> MEREDITH: It's the exact same!

CRISTINA: No, it's not. You and McDreamy are in a relationship.

MEREDITH: And you and Burke are in. . . ?

CRISTINA: Switzerland. It's very neutral there. ("Raindrops Keep Falling on My Head," 2-1)

This is especially true when, after matters become less "neutral" between them, Burke insists on telling the Chief about what really is a relationship—and is given the "you're consenting adults" version of permission.

And as long as we're discussing relationships of disproportionate power, how about the Izzie/Denny pairing that emotionally dominated the second half of season two? Perhaps it was more emotionally palatable because Denny was clearly a strong man, despite his bad heart.

BAILEY: It would concern me if you're making medical decisions based on how our Dr. Stevens might feel about it.

DENNY: Well, in that case I say we do this thing. Screw that ditzy blonde doctor girl.

BAILEY: That's not helping, Denny.

DENNY: No?

BAILEY & MEREDITH: No. ("Blues for Sister Someone," 2-23)

Later in that episode, Bailey asked Meredith to tell her more: "What is going on between Stevens and Denny? Is it a crush? Is it an innocent flirtation? Or is Stevens actually crossing the line?" But on *Grey's Anatomy*, more than most other shows, "the line" is particularly difficult to see. While Izzie may be the doctor, she's easily as vulnerable as Denny, if not moreso. (Overlap!)

As their flirtation grew into love, Izzie proved exactly why their relationship was so dangerous—she convinced Denny to make a seriously unwise medical decision, to let her cut the LVAD wires to raise his status on the UNOS list and allow him to get a heart that became available. At first, he held firm to the morally "right" decision:

DENNY: Izzie . . . Izzie, stop and listen to me. We're not doing this.

IZZIE: Don't worry. You're not going to die. I will be here the whole time to make sure of that. . . .

DENNY: This isn't about me dying. All right? This is wrong.

IZZIE: You've waited a year and a half to get this thing. Who knows when the next one is going to come along?

DENNY: I'll take my chances.

IZZIE: No. It may be too late by then.

DENNY: Then it's too late. . . .

IZZIE: Denny! Please. You have to do this.

DENNY: No, Izzie! I'm not about to steal a heart from another man's chest!

Which is some damned impressive morality, considering that his life was at stake. But her desperation led to a full, sobbing breakdown:

DENNY: Izzie . . . I'm going to be all right. All right? You don't have to worry.

IZZIE: What about *me*? What about me when you go into the light?

DENNY: Izzie—

IZZIE: No! I get it, okay? I get it! You'll be okay, you'll be fine, but what about me? So don't do it for yourself, do it for me! Please? Please, Denny! Please do this for me! Because if you die—you have to do this! You have to do this for me, or I'll never be able to forgive you!

DENNY: For dying?

IZZIE: No! *For making me love you!* Please do this for me? Please! Do this for me! Please?!

DENNY: Okay. Okay, I'll do it. ("17 Seconds," 2-25)

It is absolutely wrong, *and it is wholly believable.* Something Denny wouldn't consider to save his life, he would still do for Izzie. In the end, Izzie and Denny paid the price for her desperate plan. They paid dearly. And Izzie took full responsibility, despite that her friends did their best

175

to cover for her: "It was me. I cut his LVAD wire. I did it, no one helped me. And now . . . I thought I was a surgeon, but I'm not, so I quit" ("Losing My Religion," 2-27). Even when they did wrong—by the clear-cut standards, anyway—nobody seemed especially villainous.

If you watch the series closely, you'll see dozens of other examples in which characters make decisions that some people—and some shows—might use either to preach against or to justify, or to falsely simplify, certain agendas. When Cristina found herself pregnant, she didn't hesitate about getting an abortion, an action prevented only when her ectopic pregnancy made the decision moot. Nobody (with the possible exception of a clinic nurse who counseled further consideration) judged her for it. In contrast, when a patient arrived at Seattle Grace pregnant with her seventh child, and asked Addison to tie her tubes without telling her very Catholic husband, the issue of secrecy was debated by Addison and Alex. But nobody questioned the patient's right to have seven children if she wanted them and could care for them. Her family's decisions were their own to make, as Cristina's were hers. Meredith's series of nameless lovers, after she broke up with Derek, were questioned only as they indicated an unhealthy pattern, not a moral deviance. And even the "terrible thing" that Meredith did to George—sleeping with him, then weeping and asking if he was almost done—was not done maliciously. As discussed much later:

> GEORGE: Why? I just want to know why you. . . . If you did-n't want to—
> MEREDITH: I didn't know I didn't want to. . . . You were there and you were saying all these perfect things and I was sad. And so I thought maybe, maybe I've just been overlooking what's been in front of me. And if I just give it a chance because you're George and you're so great. . . . I didn't know I didn't want to until I knew I didn't want to. ("What Have I Done to Deserve This?," 2-19)

In true *Grey's* fashion, the responsibility didn't really weigh on only one person's head anyway. As George told Meredith, in "Deterioration of the Fight or Flight Response" (2-26):

> You wanna know something? I knew. I knew you didn't feel that way about me, even during—when we were in bed, I knew. I knew and I still let it happen, because, um, well, I figured that one night with you was better than never. So, will you just stop saying that you're sorry? Cause you didn't know any better, but I did. And . . . I'm sorry. I'm sorry, Meredith.

True, there are still some clear lines of "black and white" moral demarcation, even in *Grey's Anatomy*. The violent rapist was clearly a bad guy. A woman who devoted her life to helping dozens of people, including Chief Webber, to overcome their addiction to alcohol was clearly a good guy. As Cristina noted about Meredith sleeping with George: "He's the weaker kid. I mean, I don't even beat up on weaker kids" ("What Have I Done to Deserve This?," 2-19). But there are far more gray areas in which the difference between good guy and bad guy overlap. In "Damage Case" (2-24), a pregnant young woman was injured when a surgical intern fell asleep at the wheel—clearly his fault. When the characters were introduced, the injured woman's burly hick of a father, Big Jim, was outraged: "I'll kill him! You son of a bitch!" But by the end of the episode, after the daughter died in surgery, the driver whose unintentional negligence had killed her tearfully apologized to her father . . . and Big Jim, eyes wild with grief and fury, patted him on the shoulder, touched his face, comforted him.

177

Even he knew that some things are not that clear-cut, even when we want them to be. The recognition of that affects us far more deeply than simplistic morality tales ever could.

In the Emmy-nominated two-parter that first won me over to the show, "It's the End of the World" and "(As We Know It)" (2-16 and 2-17), the character of Hannah did something awful. Knowing that moving her hand—which was inside a patient, holding an explosive device—could blow up the entire OR, she nevertheless panicked, pulled loose, and ran. But she was no simple coward. She'd only been on the job for two weeks. She was left alone, even by the anesthesiologist who delivered a grim speech about how, when blown up, people become "pink mist." And, despite her panicked flight, Hannah stayed in the hospital, despite the threat of explosion, to find out what happened, even though she could have kept running. It seemed only fitting that by the end, as Hannah lurked miserably by the nurse's desk, Burke pointed her out as the woman who should be thanked for the patient's survival.

Too much of a clear-cut paradigm of cowardice vs. bravery, of good vs. bad, is just too simplistic for *Grey's Anatomy*.

CHARACTER AMBIGUITY

But it's not only in dualism of right and wrong (and the seemingly endless space in between) that *Grey's Anatomy* refuses to over-simplify. It's in the show's greatest strength, the characters themselves. These people are clearly drawn; I'm not implying that their basic personalities change to suit the needs of each individual episode, because they don't. But neither are their basic personalities that . . . basic. Almost all of them have unexpected layers.

Take Miranda Bailey, for example. She is one tough, drill-sergeant style character, introducing herself with the following words:

178

> I have five rules, memorize them. Rule number one: Don't bother sucking up. I already hate you. That's not gonna change. . . . You're interns, grunts, nobodies; bottom of the surgical food chain. You run labs, write orders, work every second night until you drop, and don't complain. ("A Hard Day's Night," 1-1)

She is seriously good at what she does, both in surgery and in corralling her "suck-ups." Even after almost two seasons of getting to know these interns—and one of them, George, helping her deliver her child—Bailey remains gruffly, solidly *Bailey*. When Meredith started to tell her about her possible date with a veterinarian, Bailey asked, "Grey, do you actually believe that I care?"

> MEREDITH: No.
> BAILEY: Good. Maybe you're not so stupid after all. ("Blues
>   for Sister Someone," 2-23)

Which is about as close as she comes to a compliment. And yet, despite her seeming indifference, as well as taking a hard line against Meredith and Derek's forbidden romance, with Bailey's strength comes a strong protective instinct. After Derek's wife appeared on the scene, he wanted to go see if Meredith is okay, but Bailey ran blockade:

> She's not [okay]. She's a human traffic accident and everybody is slowing down to look at the wreckage. She's doing the best she can with what she has left. Look, I know you can't see this because you're in it. But you can't help her now, it'll only make it worse. Now walk away and leave her to mend. ("Something to Talk About," 2-7)

Not exactly the words of a hard-ass. Rather, they're the words of a hard-ass who uses her powers for good, as when she told off the obnoxious manager of a shot-up restaurant in "17 Seconds" (2-25) because his employees were afraid of losing their jobs. Bailey's not all one extreme or the other—she's a mixture.

179

If the example of the gruff-leader-with-a-heart-of-gold doesn't seem quite original enough to convince you of *Grey's* brilliance, take a look at George O'Malley. George starts as the sweet-but-dumpy loser guy. In the first episode, we learned that he may still live with his mother (something he rectified only by moving in with Meredith and Izzie). His fumbling during his first procedure earned him the initial loser nickname of "007" (as in "License to Kill"). He loved Meredith from afar, but she never seemed to notice him. He started dating a nurse, only to get syphilis—which, it turned out, she got from dating the cocky intern Alex, a clear alpha male to George's beta. Meredith said of him in the second episode, "The First Cut is the Deepest" (1-2), "You are such a woman." They were cooing over babies at the time.

If being overly sensitive or coming out on the losing side was all George was about, he would still be a decent character. Sweet. Harmless. The Neville Longbottom of Seattle Grace. But *Grey's Anatomy* rarely rests on such simplicity. True, even Harry Potter's Neville has his moments of foundering glory. But George's moments of glory rarely even founder. When he learned that his syphilis originated from Alex, George gave him a black eye . . . so gee, maybe George isn't a coward. In fact, George is often surprisingly brave, especially when it comes to the courage of his own convictions. George refused to report to the Chief all the gossip he stumbled across when Webber, bed-ridden from recent brain surgery, ordered George to soak up all the goings-on like a sponge and report back to him. George is the one who forced a pregnant Bailey to snap out of her panic when her husband's automobile accident led to her refusal to have the baby that was ready to be born:

> GEORGE: Dr. Bailey, I'm surprised at you. I really thought—this is not how I thought you would do this.
> ADDISON: Dr. O'Malley, I don't think that—
> GEORGE: I truly—I expected more.
> ADDISON: George.
> GEORGE: You're Dr. Bailey. You don't hide from a fight. You don't give up. You strive for greatness. You, Dr. Bailey, you are a doer. And . . . I know your husband is not here and I know that there are a lot of things going on here that we have no control over. But this, we can do. Okay? Okay. Let's have this baby. ("[As We Know It]," 2-17)

180

All this, against the protests of both his immediate boss (Bailey) and her boss (Addison). Both Chief Weber and Derek Shepherd recoiled from a glimpse of Bailey in the stirrups getting her cervix examined, soon after her water broke—"a visual image I'll never get out of my head," complained Derek ("It's the End of the World," 2-16). George, in contrast, was there through her entire labor and delivery, so enthralled by the miracle of birth that Bailey herself had to order him (now famously) to "Stop lookin' at my va-*jay*-jay" ("[As We Know It]," 2-17).

Not enough? George forged ahead in finding some way the hospital could help cover the expenses for bartender Joe's very expensive but life-saving stand-still operation, despite Chief Webber's insistence that this was not part of their responsibility as a hospital. When trapped with Alex in an elevator, with a patient having cardiac arrest, it was George who stayed calm and followed Dr. Burke's relayed instructions to perform open-heart surgery and save the man's life. In the earlier example about Bex, George is the one who insisted on his patient's right to know the truth about her hermaphroditism. And George, from a pro-union household, refused to cross the nurses' picket line despite the threat to his own advancement . . . until the nurses themselves convinced him to please go inside and secretly check on particularly difficult patients, a decision that helped highlight the paradox that is George. He's not weak. He's not a coward. He just *cares*. He cares so much that he often hesitates, to make sure that he's doing the right thing, to make sure he's not stepping on other people's wants or needs. So in a culture that embraces tough-guy alpha males, he sometimes appears weak.

But not to everyone. As Izzie says of Callie, in "The Name of the Game" (2-22), "Oh my God. George is her McDreamy."

Bailey and George may be the stand-outs, but the same points can be made about numerous other characters. Cristina Yang, for example, usually comes across as tough, driven, and not particularly sympathetic of others. She's chosen surgery because "Surgery's hot. It's the marines. It's macho. It's hostile. It's hardcore" ("A Hard Day's Night," 1-1). When Meredith complained about her new roommates, Izzie and George, Cristina's suggestion was simple and surgical:

181

> CRISTINA: Kick them out.
> MEREDITH: I can't kick them out, they just moved in. I asked them to move in.
> CRISTINA: So what, you're just going to repress everything in some deep, dark, twisted place until one day you snap and you kill them?
> MEREDITH: Yep.
> CRISTINA: This is why we are friends. ("Winning a Battle, Losing the War," 1-3)

For heaven's sake—Cristina once said of babies, "They make you toxic" ("The First Cut is the Deepest," 1-2). And yet she's the same Cristina who recoiled from helping her lover, Dr. Burke, make a career-defining decision about surgery to fix his injured hand, in "Deterioration of the Fight or Flight Response" (2-26). She's the same Cristina who began to weep when grilled by Dr. Webber about who cut Denny's LVAD wire, not because she was afraid of disciplinary action, but because she was confused by how badly her interpersonal relationships had complicated her usually ruthless drive:

> I had an edge, Sir. I had an edge, and I've lost it. And I need it. I need it back. So . . . if you could just tell me . . . how you keep yours . . . and how not to be affected? ("Losing My Religion," 2-27)

Another character with surprising shades of gray is the initially abrasive Alex Karev. Early in the series, Alex called George "gay" and Izzie "Dr. Model":

> ALEX: Morning, Dr. Model.
> IZZIE: Dr. Evil Spawn.
> ALEX: Ooh, nice tat. Do they airbrush that out for the catalogs?
> IZZIE: I don't know. What do they do for the 666 on your skull? ("No Man's Land," 1-4)

He plastered the locker room with enlargements of Izzie's lingerie spreads from the "Bethany Whisper" catalog. Although he was sweet to tumor patient Annie in order to charm her and get in on the case in "If Tomorrow Never Comes" (1-6), he reverted to form as soon as he thought she couldn't hear him:

> I mean, man, that is a whole lot of nasty! . . . Please. If you're afraid of doctors, you take a pill. She's just sick, like, warped, you know? Seriously, I don't know how she lives with herself.

Alex alienated Burke by trash-talking about a patient's chances while the patient was on the operating table—admittedly unconscious. He alienated Addison the OB-GYN with his reluctance to be part of her "vagina squad." He made numerous cruel jokes about Denny's chances of dying after Izzie chose the heart patient over him. And yet even Alex can't be relegated to one simple side of the moral spectrum. He explained it best himself, in "The Name of the Game" (2-22), when Burke chewed him out for telling a dying woman that she's doing her daughter no favors by hiding her own imminent death:

> I tell the truth. It's what I do. It doesn't make me a bad doctor. Maybe I'm a pig, maybe I'm an ass, maybe I'm a vermin like everybody says. But I tell them the truth. It's the one thing that I've got going for me, and you don't get to take that away and call it a lesson. Sir.

Just as important? It turns out he was right. The dying mother found the courage to admit the truth to her daughter, and had a chance to give their relationship closure: "You're going to feel sad for a little while, and that's okay. But don't feel sad forever, okay? Will you promise me that?" It's a truly touching moment—and it was made possible by the honesty of Dr. Evil Spawn, the pig-ass vermin. Of course, Alex's finest moment to date came after Denny's death, at the end of season two. Despite Izzie's violent, grief-stricken refusal to let anybody touch her, much less pry her from her dead fiancé, Alex—jilted, jealous Alex—was the one brave enough to draw her away.

> Iz, that's not Denny. The minute his heart stopped beating he stopped being Denny. Now I know you love him, but he also loved you. And a guy who loves you like that, he doesn't want you to do this to yourself. Because it's not Denny. Not anymore. ("Losing My Religion," 2-27)

It may be a harsh truth. But truth it is—and all the more powerful for coming not from a normal show's limited cast of "good guys" but from a character as complex, and as ambiguous, as so much else in *Grey's Anatomy*.

So . . . *Grey's Anatomy* isn't simplistic. It isn't dualistic. It doesn't push a false dichotomy of black or white, good or bad, male or female, and it doesn't embrace arbitrary rules. Instead, it lingers in the far more complicated overlap between the simplistic extremes, forcing the audience to think—and to enjoy it, too. *Grey's* delivers, on a weekly basis, a view of life that's messy, and beautiful, and complicated, and full of shades of gray. And I suspect I'm not the only one who finds that appealing. But why?

Maybe the late Denny said it best when defending his "forbidden" love for his doctor, Izzie:

> The thing is, I was healthy my whole life 'til I wasn't. And for the last year, I've had a lot of time to lay around in bed and think about my life. And the things I remember best? Well, those are the things that I wasn't supposed to do and I did 'em anyway. So the thing is . . . life is too damn short to be following these rules. ("Blues for Sister Someone," 2-23)

The show certainly proved him right, and continues to prove him right, again and again. The way that *Grey's* soars above other, also strong shows, is that its deliciously ambiguous characters refuse to be defined by rules, by extremes, by clear-cut labels.

Maybe that's one reason lucky viewers will remember *Grey's Anatomy* best, as well.

184

Rita Award-winning author EVELYN VAUGHN has published sixteen romance and adventure novels (including *A.K.A. Goddess* and *Lost Calling*), and a dozen fantasy short stories in anthologies such as *A Constellation of Cats*, *Vengeance Fantastic*, and *Familiars*. She also teaches literature and creative writing for Tarrant County College, in Texas. When neither writing nor teaching . . . oh, who are we kidding? She's almost always writing and teaching. And watching TV (being an addict). It helps her rest up from the writing. And the teaching. She loves to talk about her writing (and TV), whether that's attractive or not. Check out her Web site at www.evelynvaughn.com.

How can we explain *Grey's Anatomy's* phenomenal success? The characters? The storylines? The simple draw of hot doctors having lots of inappropriate sex? Patrick Dempsey's hair? No, says Kevin Smokler, it's more than all that—it's timing.

Kevin Smokler

ANATOMY OF TWENTY-FIRST CENTURY TELEVISION

There's no logical reason why I love *Grey's Anatomy*. I'm not a woman and don't understand why the show gets labeled a chick program. I have no interest in medicine even though I went to Johns Hopkins. I don't live in Seattle, was not a fan of any of the actors before the series, and by the time you read this, will have exited television's mythic 18–34 demographic. But I'm an addict, addicted enough to have watched both seasons live, on TiVo-ed repeat, *and* on DVD. I even got my parents hooked. Last fall when I went to visit them, my flight landed during the premiere of *Grey's* third season. They refused to pick me up at the airport.

How did this happen? None of the usual suspects—compelling characters, sassy dialogue, Patrick Dempsey's hair—quite get to it. Deep down I think *Grey's* and I have shacked up for much less sexy reasons, the kind I'd employed years ago to hit on women as a graduate student in American Studies. Only in this case, it worked.

Grey's Anatomy is a member of the first graduating class of twenty-first century television. In both form and content, the program and its fellows—*Lost, Desperate Housewives, CSI, 24*—represent our collective mindset during the opening years of the millennium just as *M*A*S*H* acted as a hangover cure for Vietnam and *Dallas* showcased the empty glamour of the Reagan era. *Grey's Anatomy's* influence extends beyond its hour on Thursday nights and tells us something about how we as a society are living now.

Call it overblown, but I love crap like that. I can watch the show for all the obvious reasons and still call my friends afterward and blather about zeitgeist mining and intertextuality. It's like discovering lemon bars are also high in fiber.

You may not be the kind of *Grey's* viewer who thinks too hard about the social relevance of it all. That probably means you're happier and better adjusted than I. But I've never been the kind of fan who watches television to "escape." I escape by taking a nap. I get sucked into a program not because of characters and only sometimes because of plot. What my favorite shows all have in common is a big neon "WHY" in their front windows. Why am I watching *this* program instead of dozens of others on the schedule? Why do I love this show *now*, as a professional in my early thirties, and would I have as a teenager or a retiree? Most important, why does its success appear to say something about our national psyche beyond "there's always room for quality television," especially since there usually isn't?

Awareness of their place in time separates the shows that get on the cover of *Time* magazine (those crowned "a cultural phenomenon") from those that grace *TV Guide* (an honor connected to high ratings). *Frasier*, *Everybody Loves Raymond*, and *Home Improvement* all made mad bank for their networks. But thirty years from now, they won't be remembered as much more than nostalgia, hour fillers on TV Land or its futuristic equivalent. In contrast, programs such as *All in the Family*, *The Mary Tyler Moore Show*, *The Cosby Show*, and *The Simpsons* sit on dual thrones as great entertainment and cultural mileposts. Archie Bunker, Mary Richards, the Huxtables, and Homer and Marge Simpson are as much about relatability as they are personifications of our national struggle over generational change, women's liberation, the progress of racial equality, and the reshaping of the American family. Their success wasn't just about quality, but about why certain qualities were important at certain times in history.

The staff of Seattle Grace's surgery floor seem headed for this same hall of fame. For now, they're preoccupied with CT scans and sex in the sleep room. But I'm predicting their relevance will be larger than their scrubs, longer than a twenty-four-hour shift in the pit. And we'll see it if we stop for a moment and think about that neon WHY in the window.

But before we get to WHY, let's start with WHAT. What the hell is a "twenty-first century television show" besides reheated academic jargon? What makes one successful program fit to wear the sash of an era while others settle for the consolation prizes of high ratings, giant paydays, and the armload of Emmys that seem reserved for hugely popular yet ultimately forgettable programming?

First, you've probably heard that the network TV business is in upheaval, like heels-over-hotplate upheaval. Ratings have been declining for years. Cable, where curse words run free, takes larger bites out of the pie every season. TiVo and On Demand services let you skip commercials. And that thing called the Internet is on all the time, luring TV viewers, particularly younger ones, to a box of a very different kind. Out in the real world, America is in an anxious haze about its own safety, juggling work, family, and personal happiness with only partial success and trading mass individualism (iPod playlists, Netflix queues) as cultural currency much more than communal experience (tell me about the last Fourth of July parade you went to).

A twenty-first century television show therefore showcases these issues at work in the lives of its characters and, by extension, those who watch them. *Grey's Anatomy* accomplishes this brilliantly through five of its unique characteristics: its use of the program as a multimedia platform, success as both niche and mass entertainment, its sense of place and placelessness and the blurring of the borders between work and play, and the show's emphasis on ethnic diversity.

I.

It's an open secret these days that you can't just put a show on TV and wait for viewers to show up. You can't even really hype it the old-fashioned way (commercials, billboards, subway posters), because we've grown so accustomed to advertising that we scarcely notice it anymore. Plus, with cell phone Tetris, Blackberry flirting, and hundreds of other digitized distractions, television that succeeds in the twenty-first century must be everywhere you are. Often, that's not sitting in front of the set.

Adding to that, the holy grail of any television show is a dedicated following that can't get enough of the program and wants to devote ungodly amounts of time to yapping about it, writing fan fiction about minor characters, and creating ring tones from the show's theme song. It's in that show's best interest to stoke these obsessions but not give over to them, to give fans enough to satisfy their hunger yet keep them wanting more. And with the intimacy and transparency provided by participatory media, this has never been easier.

The minds behind *Grey's Anatomy* get this. They take what's normally background and backstage about network television and invite their fans inside it. The result is that *Grey's* feels less like a product trading hands and more like a place where both creators and audience hang out together.

Take music. In the 1990s, *Beverly Hills, 90210* and *Friends* demonstrated that TV shows, like movies, could have soundtracks. Until the last few years, however, most were essentially souvenir-stand items for the faithful, a hodgepodge of songs heard in the background of show episodes or "suggested" by the program itself. Music wasn't really integral to a TV show but rather a deliverable marketed by slapping the show's name on it.

188

Thanks first to *Dawson's Creek* and later *The O.C.*, music and TV now have a more symbiotic relationship. Lesser-known acts can get their first national exposure on a popular series. By featuring their music (which can be used much more cheaply than chart-topping hits), TV shows can brand themselves tastemakers and attract an audience looking to get ahead of the cultural curve.

The music on *Grey's Anatomy* is not only ubiquitous (*Grey's* has been criticized for having sonic diarrhea; no argument here), but almost a separate platform through which fans can interact with the show. ABC has released two volumes of soundtracks—at the ridiculously quick pace of one for each year on the air—made up of songs easily identified with the program's big moments, instead of off-the-shelf tunes by bands the show would like to link itself with (Hootie & the Blowfish's "I Go Blind" was added to an episode of Friends about a H&TB concert to coincide with the release of the soundtrack). *Grey's* favorite bands skew gently alternative (you may not have heard of them, but your cooler friend in a Neighborhoodie already calls them passé) and are often suggested by the writers themselves, who blog about their own local music outings at Grey Matter (www.greyswriters.com), the show's official writers' blog. Immediately following an episode, fans scurry to Web sites such as TV.com or Television Without Pity to identify music they heard and liked. ABC.com also provides a searchable guide of the music featured in each episode. Downloading at varying levels of legality ensue.

Thus the music on *Grey's* not only helps label the show for a certain kind of viewer (savvy but willing to be schmaltzed, hip but politely so), but also keeps talk of *Grey's* humming long after the episode is over. Every time Joe Purdy's "The City" pops up on your iPod, you think of Meredith breaking it off with Derek outside his trailer. That it happens via a completely separate medium reveals that the minds behind *Grey's Anatomy* understand the liquidity of contemporary culture and the attention arms race of twenty-first century media: A television show isn't just a block of time once a week; it can't be. Your fans might not be available during that hour. Instead, it is an introduction to a world of affiliated culture and media, a lifestyle choice you can drape over your shoulders and wear around.

Grey Matter is the same story. The writing staff of the show post an average of four times a week to the blog during the season and about half that over the summer. That a hugely successful network show has its writers blogging is forward-thinking enough (or would have been in 2001; it's right on schedule for a large media conglomerate), but two other things stand out—what they blog about and how fans respond. Let's look at this post from September 28, 2006, by writer Krista Vernoff, who penned the third season's second episode:

> I love McSteamy. I loved him when I introduced you to him in "Yesterday" and I love him even more when he's standing in a towel at the end of this episode. I wrote it. I saw the dailies when it was shot. And still, when I first watched the cut, my jaw dropped with giddy surprise when I saw him emerge from that bathroom. Love me my McSteamy. . . . Okay,

also? I love Izzie in this episode. . . . As for Meredith, my inner single girl is flippin' jealous. Cause really—did you see that bar scene? With McVet walking in all slo-mo and hot and then McDreamy doing the same damn thing.

Where's the pretentious nonsense about "character arc"? Where are the coy bromides about "producing quality television for a quality audience," and where is the long hand of a network exec editing it within an inch of its life? Nowhere. The writers sound like the audience. Their posts are chatty, flip, and, well, human. There's no mention of an agent's new BMW or whom they had lunch with at the Ivy. It's like talking about the show with your friends, except "your friends" not only watch the show with you but also make it happen.

The fans then jump in and comment, an average of about 700 per post in the week I looked at. The writers usually don't participate much beyond their original posting, but it hardly matters because they've already set the tone of the conversation. Where the old model of television production resembled an ultimatum (we make, you watch), *Grey's* has transformed it into a gab session (we make, you watch, then we all talk about it together). If *Inside the Actor's Studio*, DVD extras, and podcasts from the set (T. R. Knight, who plays George O'Malley, does one for *Grey's*) are any indication, fans want to interact with their favorite entertainers, not just passively consume their product. Grey Matter creates a sense of intimacy between the biggest TV show in the land and, conceivably, thousands of its fans, a feat that seems both impossible and relentlessly now. *Grey's Anatomy* gets that, when the audience has a million options besides yours, the best strategy is to host the conversation, not dominate it.

II.

Remember *The Daily Show* before Jon Stewart hosted—because, yes, there was another host? Remember that *Grey's Anatomy* was a mid-season replacement in 2005, not a splashy fall debut with a ton of money and hype behind it? Raging success tends to obscure humble beginnings.

Miraculously, *Grey's* has managed to hang onto the spirit of its quiet birth even as its popularity grew. Its season three debut garnered over 30 million viewers, and yet I speak to fellow TV addicts every day who have never watched the show. *Grey's* has spawned no catchphrases on the order of *Seinfeld's*. "Not that there's anything wrong with that." Cast members haven't shown up in Pepsi commercials. The show's creator, Shonda Rhimes, is nearly as famous as the actors (which is almost unheard of. How many of us know what Aaron Sorkin looks like? Or what Larry David did before *Curb Your Enthusiasm?*). *Grey's Anatomy* feels like your secret pleasure that, by the way, 30 million other people enjoy as well.

How this happens is an inscrutable tangle of luck, discipline, and attitude, but this much is clear: Niche is the new mainstream, and *Grey's Anatomy* personifies it. As laid out in Chris Anderson's seminal study "The Long Tail," "the future of business is selling less of more." In media terms, this means that a thousand niche audiences can add up to larger fortunes than one or two mile-wide, inch-deep audiences. And with TiVo and now iTunes, success isn't just about grabbing the largest possible audience on a specific night of the week and serving them up to the largest advertisers. Loyal fans will now self-identify through paid downloads and Season Passes. From there, a show can either grow bigger, as *Grey's Anatomy* has done, or stay with its hopefully desirable, dedicated small audience and charge advertisers accordingly. Either way, it's likely the success of *Grey's* is already being laid out on the examination table. How does it manage to be everyone's show and only yours at the same time? We may not know yet, but it looks like the answer will influence how networks produce television long after the interns at Seattle Grace have graduated from the program and moved on.

191

III.

Let's talk location. *Grey's Anatomy* takes place in Seattle, but I've yet to find someone who can tell me why. Creator Shonda Rhimes is from Chicago and has never lived in the Pacific Northwest. There are no line drops about Starbucks, Microsoft, or Kurt Cobain. Neighborhoods are rarely mentioned by name, and local gems such as the Fremont Troll are studiously ignored. Aside from a few establishing shots of the Space Needle and the name of the hospital, *Grey's Anatomy* could take place in any city large enough to support a surgical internship program and near enough to water that it wouldn't have to edit out McDreamy's love of ferry boats.

This isn't surprising. Place is a slippery concept for shows on the parade float of our era. A decade ago, nineties standard bearers such as *Seinfeld, Homicide: Life on the Street, Beverly Hills, 90210,* and *Melrose Place* milked their locations with both hands. Regionalism informed how the characters dressed and spoke and fueled what made the show funny or dramatic. Can you picture the Soup Nazi setting up shop in Houston, or dead bodies in the Melrose Place pool frozen during a Detroit winter?

Today that isn't the case. *Lost* is set on a nameless island, *Desperate Housewives* in the suburban caricature of Wisteria Lane. *CSI* makes some hay from the sin and vice so much a part of Las Vegas, but the heart of the show is a laboratory. *24* rarely leaves Los Angeles but, at best, it's an uncommon L.A., one of warehouse loading docks, airport landing strips, and government office buildings. It could just as easily be Phoenix.

Why does place matter so little in today's most important TV shows, including *Grey's Anatomy*? Because it matters less to us and our mobile, restless culture. When an office can be a cell phone and a laptop, when cities look increasingly like one another, and when the Internet creates a second, non-geographic reality, how much do we really value where on the map our favorite characters live and work? About as much as we value where we do.

In the case of *Grey's Anatomy*, the show's premise is a red herring that still makes the point. Surgical interns spend their lives in a hospital, catching a few hours of sleep at home. Small wonder the show's geography seems cramped and nondescript. Maybe the lack of Seattleness in *Grey's* Seattle isn't anything more than that and has nothing to do with the zeitgeist.

But look at it this way: While not all of us work surgical intern hours, we all face the challenge of balancing our job with the rest of our life, and *Grey's Anatomy* has been about the tangling of work and personal life since its inception. The original title sequence featured seamless dissolves between medical equipment and two people preparing for and on a date. Before Dr. Addison Montgomery-Shepherd entered the picture in season two, the source of Meredith and Derek's romantic tension (and Cristina and Burke's) was their relationship as intern and medical resident. Who got this surgery or that patient came down to who was sleeping with whom and which other of them disapproved. And while patients aren't often metaphors for the show's personal dramas (unlike, say, the court cases in *Ally McBeal*), how they affect relationships between the characters is always more important than the medicine being practiced. When Tavis Smiley asked Ms. Rhimes if TV needed another medical drama her answer was quick: "To me it's not so much about medicine as it is about surgery and job competition. It's also very much about their personal lives."

In the twenty-first century, the boundaries between our work and our personal lives are blurrier than ever. We shave and apply makeup during our commute. Our offices have beds and foosball tables to make them feel more like home. Mobile phones, instant messaging, and Blackberries allow our job to follow us on vacation. Sleep is the only thing we spend more hours on than work, and that balance is shifting rapidly. If *Grey's Anatomy* is really a show about relationships, it's about relationships under the constant pressure of the contemporary workplace.

193

IV.

It's become almost a cliché to call *Grey's Anatomy* the model of culturally diverse television programming. The attention paid to creator Shonda Rhimes (profiled recently in *The New York Times*, a treatment none of the actors on the show have received) has spurred this, along with her now-frequently repeated story of attempting color-blind casting and having agents only send her white actors. "We had to call back and say, 'Where are the actors of color?'" she told Tavis Smiley on his PBS program. "And they would say 'Oh, so this is a diverse role.' And I said, 'They're all diverse roles.'"

It's a simple explanation that reveals more about the show than perhaps even its creator intended. Carrying a torch first lit by crime shows such as *Hill Street Blues* and *Law & Order*, as well as workplace dramas such as *ER*, *Grey's Anatomy* has taken ethnic diversity one step further.

We're about two decades in from television drama having one or two characters of color and having, as Ms. Rhimes put it in *The New York Times*, "a weird obligation to make that person slightly saintly because they are representing all the people of color." We're a little less than that in from having the race of those characters milked incessantly for drama (*L.A. Law* had two attorneys of color who had to shoulder most of the discrimination-centered plots), and we're still using geography as reasoning for diversity: It's difficult to have a show aim for "gritty realism" set in a large urban area and feature an all-white cast.

The multiculturalism of *Grey's Anatomy* seems to represent less demographic meddling (although it took conscious effort for it to happen at all) and more of an acceptance of contemporary conditions. Along with *Lost*, *Grey's* seems to be saying that in the twenty-first century, an assortment of people in any given situation (for *Grey's* a big city hospital, for *Lost* a transcontinental flight) will produce a mixed palette rather than a single- or two-toned one. And here, geography works to bring the point home. Our popular image of Seattle (minus perhaps the novels of Sherman Alexie) is a white one—grunge music, REI, Bill Gates—and often ignores the city's large Asian and Native American populations. *Grey's* not only quietly says that image is inaccurate (27 percent of Seattle is not white), but offers an alternative not as an exception but as a reflection of reality.

One could argue that since Ms. Rhimes is African-American and each of the characters in positions of authority are as well, that she simply played favorites in casting. But that's missing the point. Like the citizens of Seattle, one in four Americans identifies as non-white. America is no more an all-white country than Hollywood is (at least on the talent side) an all-white business. The same cannot be said for show runners in Ms. Rhimes's position, where non-white, non-men are a rarity. But signing a two-year $10 million deal with ABC hopefully makes Ms. Rhimes and her show not only a showcase of where we are now (in an America writer Richard Rodriguez has labeled "neither black nor white but varying shades of brown"), but an indicator of the kind of television and television industry to come.

It's possible that *Grey's Anatomy* could betray the trust it has built up, lose a featured player to contract dispute, or jump the shark in any number of ways. Making successful television is a high-wire act in a big top

194

filled with wind machines. Making television with an impact on the culture instead of just its studio's balance sheet is harder still. By my conservative calculations, *Grey's* will need a successful glide into syndication (Lifetime? Bravo?) as well as three more seasons on the air before it can take aim at the history books. But I can see how it will get there, which is why I show up each week, looking for a glimpse of how we live now, and, as a bonus, a new take on Patrick Dempsey's hair.

———————————

KEVIN SMOKLER is the editor of *Bookmark Now: Writing in Unreaderly Times* (Basic Books), which was a *San Francisco Chronicle* Noteable Book of 2005. His writing has appeared in the *Los Angeles Times*, the *San Francisco Chronicle*, *Fast Company*, and on National Public Radio. He lives in San Francisco and is currently at work on a second book.

REFERENCES

Anderson, Chris. *The Long Tail: Why the Future of Business Is Selling Less of More.* New York: Hyperion, 2006.

Ogunnaike, Lola. "Grey's Anatomy Creator Find Success in Surgery." *The New York Times*, 28 Sep. 2006.

Rhimes, Shonda. Interview by Tavis Smiley. *Tavis Smiley*, PBS, 28 Mar. 2005. <http://www.pbs.org/kcet/tavissmiley/archive/200503/20050328.html>

Vernoff, Krista. "Krista Vernoff on Blogging and 'I Am a Tree'." *Grey Matter*. 28 Sep. 2006. <http://www.greyswriters.com/2006/09/krista_vernoff_.html>

ACKNOWLEDGMENTS

Thanks to Adam of The Seriously Grey Area
for assistance with the manuscript
(http://theseriouslygreyarea.com).